Making Sense of Subsidiarity: How Much Centralization for Europe?

Monitoring European Integration **4**

A CEPR Annual Report, 1993

The Centre for Economic Policy Research

The Centre for Economic Policy Research is a network of over 200 Research Fellows, based primarily in European universities. The Centre coordinates its Fellows' research activities and communicates their results to the public and private sectors. CEPR is an entrepreneur, developing research initiatives with the producers, consumers and sponsors of research. Established in 1983, CEPR is a European economics research organization with uniquely wide-ranging scope and activities.

CEPR is a registered educational charity. Institutional (core) finance for the Centre is provided by through major grants from the Economic and Social Research Council, the Esmée Fairbairn Charitable Trust, the Bank of England, Citibank, the Baring Foundation, 33 other companies and 14 other central banks. None of these organizations gives prior review to the Centre's publications, nor do they necessarily endorse the views expressed therein.

The Centre is pluralist and non-partisan, bringing economic research to bear on the analysis of medium- and long-run policy questions. CEPR research may include views on policy, but the Executive Committee of the Centre does not give prior review to its publications, and the Centre takes no institutional policy positions. The opinions expressed in this volume are those of the authors and not those of the Centre for Economic Policy Research.

Contributors

David Begg *Birkbeck College, London*
Jacques Crémer *Université des Sciences Sociales, Toulouse*
Jean-Pierre Danthine *Université de Lausanne*
Jeremy Edwards *St John's College, Cambridge*
Vittorio Grilli *Consiglio degli Esperti, Ministero del Tesoro, Roma*
Damien Neven *Université de Lausanne*
Paul Seabright *Churchill College, Cambridge*
Hans-Werner Sinn *Center for Economic Studies, Universität München*
Anthony Venables *London School of Economics and Political Science*
Charles Wyplosz *INSEAD, Fontainebleau*

Contents

Tables

Figures

Figures

Preface

Informed discussion of European integration should be based on economic analysis which is rigorous, yet presented in a manner accessible to public and private sector policy-makers, their advisers and the wider economic policy community. These are the objectives and the intended readership of this series of CEPR Reports.

Monitoring European Integration assesses the progress of and obstacles encountered by economic integration in Europe. A rotating panel of CEPR Research Fellows meets periodically to select key issues, analyse them in detail, and highlight the policy implications of the analysis. The output of the panel's work is a short annual Report, for which they take joint responsibility. This is the fourth in this series.

CEPR is a network of over 200 economists based in over 100 different institutions, primarily in Europe. Much of the research in the Centre's various programmes relates more or less directly to short- and long-run issues of economic policy in Europe. CEPR puts extremely high priority on effective dissemination of both policy research and the fundamental research underlying it. This series of annual Reports has become an important component of this effort. The topic for 1993 is perhaps the most challenging undertaken yet – Subsidiarity. This poorly understood concept is at the heart of current EC controversies. The prescience and relevance of previous Reports in this series promise a fresh, illuminating approach, and I believe readers will find these expectations justified.

The 1990 Report examined the impact of developments in Eastern Europe on the economies of Western Europe and on the process of economic integration among them. Some of its key insights went against conventional (and even new) wisdom, yet have proved correct and prophetic – for example, the conclusion that German unification would entail a real appreciation of the DM in the short run.

The 1991 Report dealt with Economic and Monetary Union in the European Community, in particular the macroeconomic and microeconomic issues arising from the process leading to a single currency and a European Central Bank. The Report served as an input into the discussions and the negotiations leading to the Maastricht EC summit of December 1991; as a guide to evaluating the treaty that emerged from Maastricht; and as a text for interpreting developments in the EMS since August 1992. Again, the analysis in that Report has proved far-sighted and robust.

The 1992 Report analysed the political economy of enlargement of the European Community. The Report argued that the EFTA countries' interest in the new European Economic Area (EEA) is mainly economic, and the wish of several to extend it into full EC membership is primarily political; whereas for the current EC members, the motivation is reversed – the EEA was mainly a political gesture, but there are significant economic incentives for bringing the EFTAns into the Community. The weakness of the economic motivation for the EFTAns may help to explain the difficulty of gaining popular support for accession in these countries. The picture for the Central and East European Countries (CEECs) is quite different: on economic grounds, EC membership is not realistic for a long time to come; but radically improved access to EC markets (including agriculture) is essential for the economic progress necessary to make membership feasible, and a commitment by the Community to ultimate membership would provide an important anchor for economic expectations in the CEECs and their political development. That commitment has since been given at the Copenhagen Council of June 1993.

The German Marshall Fund of the United States has again provided generous financial assistance essential to the completion of the Report. We are also grateful to the UK Department of Trade and Industry; to the Commission of the European Communities, whose Stimulation Plan for Economic Science financed the Centre's research network on 'Market Structure, Industrial Organization and Competition Policy'; and to the Ford Foundation, which has supported much of the Centre's research in international economics. This Report includes new research, but since it is written and published quickly so as to be relevant to ongoing policy processes, it must rest on a solid base of past fundamental and policy-oriented research. The authors and CEPR express their continuing thanks for the support of such research which has come from these bodies and all others that contribute to the Centre's funding.

The authors and CEPR are also grateful to officials in several countries and in the European Commission who were generous with their time and cooperation in discussing the issues treated here. For extensive data gathering they thank Anne-Catherine Chenaux, Roxana Ionici and Bernice Van Bronkhorst. For reviewing Chapter 2 and providing detailed comments and insight on legal matters they thank Georges Siotis, and for allowing extensive use of his unpublished work, they thank Michael Keen. For the production of the Report they thank Julie Deppé, David Guthrie and Kate Millward in particular, as well as other staff at CEPR whose patience and professionalism have been most helpful.

None of these institutions or individuals is in any way associated with the content of the Report. The opinions expressed are those of the authors alone, and not of these institutions to which they are affiliated nor of CEPR, which takes no institutional policy positions. The Centre is extremely pleased, however, to offer to an outstanding group of European economists this forum for economic policy analysis.

Richard Portes

1 November 1993

Executive Summary

In important respects, the EC is already a federal state. The 1986 Single European Act removed the right of veto by individual member states on a range of issues. As yet the EC has neither the institutions of a federal state nor clear procedures for deciding which powers should or should not be centralized.

The principle of subsidiarity, introduced at Maastricht, remains vague and capable of conflicting interpretations. Subsidiarity is not a blanket recommendation to decentralize, merely a presumption that operates unless a clear case can be made for centralization. Until detailed arguments for and against centralization are made, the principle of subsidiarity is therefore an incomplete guide to decisions as to where power should reside. Even when such arguments are spelled out, their implication for the appropriate location of power varies case by case.

Coordinating policies yields benefits when scale economies or spillovers between member states are important. Coordination may sometimes be achieved by collective agreement on rules that are then implemented at national level. Centralization of the powers at the EC level is necessary only when coordination is desirable but its decentralized implementation is not credible.

Centralization also has costs. By diminishing accountability it offers scope for policies to diverge from the best interests of constituent states, regions or localities. The appropriate location of power reflects the conflict between the costs and benefits of centralization. By laying the burden of proof on those wishing to centralize, subsidiarity recognizes the initial sovereignty of member states and emphasizes that problems of accountability of 'government failure' at the centre may be substantial.

The mobility of taxable factors between EC countries can create significant spillovers, which is potentially a powerful argument for centralization to limit the adverse effect of fiscal competition between member states. We draw three main conclusions:

First, high capital mobility within the EC undermines the taxation of capital income by member states. One solution is to centralize such taxation. A better solution to taxation of companies is to switch to a cash-flow tax which, by limiting fiscal spillovers from capital taxation, may still be designed at the national level.

Second, labour mobility is probably not yet sufficient to warrant centralization of income tax and social security policy at the EC level. Even so, the welfare state is already under some pressure from fiscal competition among member states. If labour mobility became substantially greater, the welfare state could survive only by centralization.

Third, lower bounds on national rates of VAT have already been imposed, and they are an appropriate decentralized implementation of a concerted EC policy to prevent harmful fiscal competition on VAT.

Protests about social dumping primarily reflect the erosion of labour market power of particular groups as a result of integration of product and capital markets. While labour mobility remains limited, there is no strong case for centralizing social policies. Spillovers across member states are relatively small. The Social Chapter of the Maastricht Treaty directly contradicts the subsidiarity principle in that Treaty.

Arguments for centralizing EC fiscal policy for macroeconomic stabilization are unconvincing, not because stabilization is unnecessary but because the additional gains of its centralized pursuit are outweighed by the adverse incentives that centralization would entail. Fiscal stabilization at national level remains appropriate, but it is unnecessarily impeded by the Maastricht ceilings on budget deficits, which should therefore be interpreted with flexibility over the business cycle.

Our framework of analysis may also be applied to a range of other policy issues, from the environment, the CAP and regional policy, to merger policy and satellite regulation. Even within issues, the case for centralization is much weaker for some policies than for others. EC regulation of drinking water quality, for instance, is inconsistent with subsidiarity, but there is a better case for an EC role in management of problems where international spillovers are significant, such as the pollution of the Rhine. Overall, we conclude that there is a strong case for centralization in some areas that at present comprise a small share of the EC budget and an equally strong case for decentralization of areas that currently constitute a large part of the budget. There is no case at all for a Centralized Agricultural Policy.

1 Introduction

1.1 The Purpose of this Report

Subsidiarity may be the most contentious abstract noun to have entered European politics since 1789. And it is certainly the most abstract. While most readers of serious newspapers have become vividly aware in recent months that subsidiarity is important, few can have felt confident that they knew why, or even that they knew exactly what it was. It has a lot to do with decentralization, but the two concepts are not the same. Press commentators appear divided: does it mean something precise, and therefore either welcome or worrying according to your point of view? Or something vague, and therefore either reassuring or infuriating according to your point of view? Is subsidiarity something that pro- or anti-Europeans should welcome more?

This Report has been prepared by a group of ten economists from five countries in Western Europe. We began with the same sense of confusion that the term has generated, yet our discussions have produced some strong and occasionally surprising conclusions. There is no single punchline, and proponents of none of the main identifiable points of view in the current debate will find all our conclusions welcome. One thing that has become clear to us is that the ratification of the Maastricht Treaty will not end the argument: serious debate over the distribution of power in the European Community is only just beginning.

This debate is primarily about the appropriate balance of power between the institutions of the Community and those of its member states. To put it another way, it is about the extent to which the Community is, or ought to be, a federal institution. The concept of subsidiarity, which appears in Article 3b of the Maastricht Treaty, articulates a presumption that the powers of EC institutions should be limited to those functions that cannot be adequately performed by its member states. This principle has been variously hailed as a realistic practical alternative to what would otherwise be an indiscriminate process of centralization of power in the Community, and condemned as a pious principle with no hard content, designed purely to deflect criticism of this centralizing process. This Report will investigate the economic content of the subsidiarity principle and its implications for the allocation of economic power among different institutions within the European Community. We shall understand economic power very broadly as including all powers to affect the allocation of economic resources, and we consider not only the institutions of the EC itself and its existing member states but also those of other actual and potential jurisdictional units such as regions and localities.

Our investigation will require us to clarify what, precisely, the question is to which the subsidiarity principle is supposed to provide (part of) the answer. We shall then need to examine that answer in two stages. Subsidiarity presupposes that decentralized allocations of power are to be preferred unless there are good reasons for centralization. Although in some political and legal traditions decentralization needs no further justification (for instance, because it invokes considerations of the rights of individuals or communities), we shall ask why decentralization should even be considered desirable in the first place. If, as we believe, a convincing answer can be given to this in terms of its capacity to contribute to improvements in resource allocation, we shall then need to investigate what exactly might constitute 'good reasons' for overriding the presumption of decentralization in certain cases. Critics of the subsidiarity principle are right to point out that it is vacuous unless a systematic account can be given of these reasons.

The Report is structured as follows. In the remainder of this chapter we give an outline of the arguments for and against decentralization that will be explored in later chapters. *Chapter 2* describes the current allocation of powers among institutions at different levels within the European Community, and it examines the extent to which the EC already has a federal structure. Against that background, we then explore the political and legal content of the subsidiarity principle as it has been discussed to date, in order to provide a background to the subsequent arguments. *Chapter 3* will set out our basic analysis of the relationship between jurisdictions in order to determine the conditions under which a form of competition among decentralized jurisdictions can lead to a better resource allocation than a centralized pooling of powers. We evaluate the quality of resource allocation in terms of three criteria: efficiency, distributional equity and accountability of government. *Chapter 4* discusses a particularly important type of competition among jurisdictions that some have claimed would lead to an erosion of the entire welfare state: competition to attract taxpayers and deter benefit claimants, in a world where both groups may be expected to be increasingly mobile within the European Community. *Chapter 5* explores a contentious aspect of this question: is there a case for centralizing the regulation of the labour market, including wages and working conditions – in short, for a Social Europe? Or can a common labour policy be expected to do for labour markets what the Common Agricultural Policy has done for agricultural markets? *Chapter 6* looks at macroeconomic aspects of the insurance state: can stabilization policy be carried out effectively by member states, or should the Community have a role? *Chapter 7* applies our analysis of the subsidiarity question to a number of areas where the state has a regulatory role: competition policy, the environment, agriculture, regional development and industrial policy (which we illustrate with reference to the European satellite industry). *Chapter 8* concludes.

1.2 Subsidiarity: What is the Question?

The question, then, to which subsidiarity is supposed to provide part of the answer, is who or what should have the power in a modern state to

(a) levy taxes;

(b) undertake expenditure on the provision of public goods and services; and

(c) regulate the behaviour of private sector agents.

The principle of subsidiarity implies that all of these categories of power should be decentralized wherever possible. That is, they should be exercised by lower-level or more local jurisdictions unless convincing reasons can be found for assigning them to higher-level or more central jurisdictions, and the onus of proof should always be on proponents of centralization.

Four points need to be made about this statement of the principle. First, subsidiarity is not the same thing as decentralization. It is a principle for allocating power upwards as well as downwards, but it incorporates a presumption in favour of allocation downwards in case of doubt.

Second, the level at which given powers are exercised need not always be an all-or-nothing matter but usually admits of degrees. For instance, a relatively central jurisdiction might be assigned the power to determine overall levels of taxation, while the power to choose which kinds of tax to levy to meet the aggregate totals might be left to more local jurisdictions.

Third, the decentralized implementation of a policy whose basic features are decided centrally is not the same as decentralization of the power to decide what the policy should be. Decentralized implementation may imply that considerable resources are employed by the localities. But decentralized power requires that these resources be controlled by some local public choice mechanism – in other words, decentralized government. In practice, of course, the distinction between local administration and local government is also one of degree rather than kind, since even effective administration depends to some extent on the consent of those upon whom the policy is imposed.

Fourth, a policy can be applied in a way that is sensitive to different regional circumstances within a jurisdiction without involving either local administration or local government. For instance, central government may choose to give tax concessions to firms in a certain regionally-concentrated industry within the context of an entirely centrally designed and implemented policy. In practice, though, as we discuss in Chapter 3, there is often a relationship between the degree of local differentiation and the power accorded to local government.

To summarize, we need to apply the subsidiarity presumption to issues of decentralization along three dimensions: uniform versus differentiated policy design, central versus local administration and central versus local government. Our use of the 'central–local' contrast does not imply that there are only two levels to be considered; in principle, questions of subsidiarity can be raised as much about the relationships of villages to districts or districts to regions as about that of member states to the European Community. In recent months the latter question has dominated press discussion, but the following chapters will make it clear that subsidiarity raises important questions 'all the way down'.

1.3   Why Does the Burden of Proof Matter?

Whether the burden of proof lies with proponents of decentralization or of centralization may not seem an important question. True, there is a large area of uncertainty regarding many areas of allocation, where the arguments are rather finely balanced and it is hard to feel confident that one level of government rather than another should really be accorded the power. But in that case does it really matter what happens?

In fact it does. The reason is that any formal allocation of responsibilities is bound to leave many ambiguities and uncertainties, in particular regarding the way in which powers will evolve in the future (the constitutional contract will be incomplete, one might say). Many issues will be resolved by a kind of bargaining for power between levels of jurisdiction as new opportunities for exercising power arise in ways that have not been foreseen. The burden of proof will affect not just the allocation of power today (which may matter little), but also the direction in which it evolves in the future (which may matter very much, even if it is hard to anticipate today).

For instance, the powers accorded by the Single European Act to the European Community's institutions in the field of environmental protection have resulted in what is arguably a greater expansion of Community competence than was foreseen at the time of the Act, when environmental regulation was less far-reaching than it is today. To take a second example, the fact that the Commission enjoys the power to propose directives and regulations to the Council, while member states themselves have no equivalent means to mark out particular areas of activity as their own exclusive domain in a routine and inconspicuous fashion, may have tilted power in favour of the Commission in a number of areas that might not have been granted that status under a systematic appraisal. This point has been recognized by the Commission itself in its voluntary withdrawal of proposals for directives in a number of areas (the packaging of foodstuffs and allocation of radio frequencies) as well as initiatives for harmonization on such matters as vehicle number-plates, the regulation of gambling, the conditions under which animals are kept in zoos, and structures and equipment for fun-fairs and theme parks.[1]

One way to interpret the recent emphasis upon subsidiarity in political discussion is as an attempt to ensure that the bargaining power in future negotiations lies much more clearly on the side of member states than it has been perceived to do so far. Whether this is desirable is another question, which we take up in Chapters 2 and 3. In Chapter 2 we point out that in certain important respects the Community has already become a federal state, whether we like it or not: qualified majority voting has meant that member states can be overruled even on matters they consider important. The EC lacks many of the institutions that provide checks and balances against the majority's exercise of power in federal states. In these circumstances subsidiarity has much to commend it.

In Chapter 3, though, we note that many of the loudest voices in the political debate have interests that may not be those of Europe's citizens as a whole. Politicians in member states may resist centralization that diminishes their power whether this is in their citizens' interests or not (and those in EC institutions have a comparable bias in favour of central power). This makes all the more important a disinterested analysis of the merits and disadvantages of centralization in each particular case.

1.4 Centralization and Decentralization: Their General Merits

At first sight, it sometimes appears puzzling that decentralization should enjoy any presumption of superiority, at least on resource allocation grounds.[2] After all, in principle a system of centralized government ought to be able to replicate any policy undertaken by a decentralized system. For instance, if two regions in a decentralized system implement different policies owing to their different circumstances, a centralized system ought to be able to implement a single policy which is regionally differentiated in exactly the same way. And if a decentralized policy faced any difficulties of coordination or cooperation among the different autonomous jurisdictions, a centralized policy ought to be able to do strictly better. So at first sight it appears to be decentralization, not centralization, that requires justification.

Two reasons stand out why the argument we have just sketched is inadequate. First, decentralized systems may be more effective at gathering information than centralized systems. This point needs stating carefully, since it is certainly true that central governments can in theory mimic the incentives of a decentralized system even as far as information gathering is concerned. While they may have to offer substantial incentives to localities to persuade them to reveal information to which they have access, these benefits would accrue to the localities anyway under a decentralized system. One serious limitation to the power of a centralized system to gather information is the central authorities' limited commitment power and the low credibility of any promises they may make not to use such information revealed to the future disadvantage of the localities. For instance, relatively prosperous localities may be deterred from revealing their high taxable capacity in the absence of any credible promise by the central authorities not to exploit this knowledge to their disadvantage in the future; and the only credible way of making such a promise may be to grant the localities autonomy (self-government) in taxation matters. A similar problem notoriously vitiated the central planning of the former Soviet bloc economies: factory managers over-fulfilling their production norms had every reason to fear that their norms in consequence would be raised in the future, so they responded only weakly to the promise of bonuses.

This argument stresses limitations to the ability of centralized states to implement decentralized solutions. The second reason is even more fundamental and emphasizes limitations to their willingness to do so. The assertion that centralization is never less efficient than decentralization depends perilously on assuming that a centralized government will be no less responsive to the interests of all citizens than are local governments. All societies whose citizens have conflicting interests face more or less serious problems of public choice. Not only may there be no unambiguously best way to resolve these conflicts of interest, but the interests of those in power may differ systematically from those of the rest of the population, which may have only a limited capacity to constrain the activities of those in power. These problems arise at all levels of government, but their severity tends to increase with the heterogeneity of the interests of the population. And some of this heterogeneity arises from differences among rather than within localities, so a system of local government may face them in a less severe form. The more the population can sort itself according to location into groups of reasonably common interest, the more effectively it may be possible to ensure that public choice reflects these local interests.

These two arguments both claim that local government may provide a more credible way to differentiate policies according to the differing needs of local populations, because it is more accountable. They therefore provide some basis for the presumption that decentralization in the most profound sense (namely local government) is to be preferred unless the resulting competition between local jurisdictions itself results in significant misallocations of resources. Chapter 3 will discuss in greater detail the kinds of misallocation that may arise, and the extent to which they may outweigh the benefits of decentralization we have just outlined.

1.5 Rights of Control and Incompleteness of Contracts

Questions about the decentralization of power essentially concern the allocation of rights of control over various important decisions. They therefore raise issues very similar to those that arise in allocating rights of decision-making in collective activities such as running a firm. It is not possible when setting up a firm to specify in advance and in a contractually binding manner exactly what decisions should be taken by the managers in all possible circumstances that may arise. Accordingly managers will be granted general rights of control, subject to the restriction that shareholders may vote to deprive managers of these rights under the appropriate circumstances (typically by qualified majority voting at annual general meetings). Bankruptcy law provides, however, for circumstances in which these overall rights of control are taken away from shareholders and passed into the hands of creditors – namely, when the firm cannot meet its repayment commitments on existing debt. The rationale for such provisions lies in the fact that creditors will be more likely than shareholders to implement the necessarily tough actions, the threat of which is required to discipline managers from squandering creditors' resources in the first place.

The importance of allocating control rights therefore arises as a direct consequence of the impossibility of specifying contractually in advance what kinds of action should be taken in what circumstances. If one could do so it would make no difference which party undertook to take the action concerned. Instead one must ask: which party will, in the absence of a binding commitment, be most likely to act approximately as an efficient policy would require?

So, for example, one may ask why it makes sense for public transport in Toulouse to be run by an authority responsible to the Mayor and Council of Toulouse rather than by a subsidiary of the Parisian public transport authority. In either case the day-to-day running must be delegated to full-time employees who are located in Toulouse. And since their remuneration conditions and management structure can in principle be the same whichever authority runs them, it might be thought to make little difference where the ultimate authority lies. In fact the critical difference is that, since the citizens of Toulouse cannot specify in advance the right transport policy to implement in all possible circumstances, they need to be assured that the ultimate authority to intervene in the decisions of the transport agency rests in the hands of parties who are likely to have the right balance of interests at heart. The Mayor and Council of Toulouse, who reside in the city and are in daily contact with (and up for re-election by) those who use and pay for the system, are more likely to have regard to this balance than an authority in the capital that must balance many other conflicting political pressures. The Parisian Transport authority could, if it wished, implement any policy that the Toulouse authority implemented. But it would be less likely to wish in all circumstances to implement the one the affected parties would prefer.

Whether decentralized government is in fact more accountable is, of course, an empirical and not a theoretical matter. We have given some reasons for thinking it likely. But in Chapter 3 we shall also examine such evidence as exists.

1.6   Concluding Remarks

We have stressed that the centralization of power in any jurisdiction involves a fundamental trade-off. Centralization brings benefits in the form of the potential for better coordination of policies. It also involves costs, notably the risk of diminished accountability. Concern for subsidiarity in the European Community depends upon the judgement that these risks deserve to be taken more seriously than they have been so far. This Report is motivated by the view that such concern is justified but that the arguments for and against centralization should also be examined systematically and case by case. The merits of subsidiarity can only be obscured if it is interpreted as an indiscriminate attachment to decentralization at all costs.

Notes

[1] See 'Overall Approach to the Application by the Council of the Subsidiarity Principle and Article 3b of the Treaty on European Union', Conclusions of the European Council, Edinburgh, December 1992, Annex 2 to Part A.

[2] Arguments that decentralization is morally right even though inefficient are not our concern here.

2 The Allocation of Powers in the European Community

This chapter looks at the institutional and legal context within which the debate about subsidiarity is taking place in the European Community. First, it describes briefly the existing processes by which powers are allocated between the Community and its member states. Next, it examines the principle of subsidiarity as expressed in the Maastricht Treaty to see what difference the principle will make to these existing processes. Finally, it gives a short overview of the relative importance of national and European laws in a number of key areas of public policy. It compares the allocation of power between the Community and its member states with those in a number of federal states and raises questions about the future evolution of this allocation of power, to be answered in the later chapters of the Report.

Three strong conclusions emerge. First of all, the existing mechanisms for allocating power between the Community and its member states are surprisingly unclear and informal, and they do not appear to rest upon a compelling economic or legal logic. Second, the notion of subsidiarity as expressed in the Treaty will not do much to clarify matters: it too is vague and capable of multiple interpretations, and it should be regarded more as the expression of a broad political principle than a clear guide to the allocation of power. Third, the lack of coherence in the existing mechanisms of allocation is all the more surprising, and all the more disturbing, because the Community has already taken a significant and decisive step towards federation in the Single European Act of 1986. By removing the right of veto from member states over many areas of policy, it has already acquired the decision-making rules appropriate to a federal state. Furthermore, it has *already* used these rules to allocate to the Community functions similar to those exercised at federal level in many existing federations. It does not, however, possess many of the institutions that have historically accompanied these powers in the development of other federal states.

2.1 The Allocation of Competences in the European Community

In this section we describe the sometimes complex legal basis upon which the powers of the European Community are founded. Our purpose in doing so is to motivate our argument that the Community needs a clearer and more systematic set of principles governing its distribution of power. In theory, the competences of the Community are delegated from the member states (in legal jargon, they are 'derived' competences) and are limited by the objectives of the Treaty of Rome. The rule is therefore that competences belong to the member states and can be shifted to the centre.[1] This allocation of competences through delegation nevertheless provides a strong legal basis for Community competences. Delegation (in international law) amounts to a reallocation of sovereignty (see Kovar, 1990). It is only in a few areas that the Community has gained competences in its own right, namely those in which the member states cannot exercise competences on their own. The harmonization of legislation is one example.

The Treaty of Rome (with its various amendments) provides the main basis, such as it is, for the allocation of competences. It defines the primary law of the Community; it gives competences to the Community in certain specific matters and indicates a number of areas where the Community has the obligation to take action (for instance the organization of agricultural markets, competition policy, commercial and transport policy) in order to fulfil particular objectives. The Single European Act has added cohesion and the environment to this list.

In contrast with most federal states, however, there is no formal mechanism for the allocation of competences within the Community, outside the areas specifically dealt with in the Treaty. The Treaty itself neither provides a full list of areas in which the Community may exercise competence, nor even lays down the principles according to which competences may be allocated in the future. By contrast, the German *Grundgesetz* (Basic Law), for instance, states that competences in principle belong to the Länder but also provides a clear rule for delegation (Article 72). The 'Bund' may make laws for one of three reasons:

(a)   because a particular matter can not be dealt with efficiently by the various Länder;

(b)   because the law of a particular Land can affect the interests of another Land or of the whole country;

(c)   in order to preserve the homogeneity of living conditions outside the territory of a Land.

The Swiss constitution grants general powers to the cantons, provides for a specific mechanism (a majority of both the cantons and of the total population) to delegate specific competences to the federation, and establishes principles similar to those of the *Grundgesetz* which determine when delegation is appropriate. Breton (1987) emphasizes the importance of the explicit allocation of power within the Canadian federation. He also draws attention to the need for institutions capable of resolving allocative conflicts in order to accommodate changing circumstances, a point we take up in Section 2.5 below.

In the absence of an explicit rule, one of the provisions in the Treaty of Rome (namely Article 235) has been used to justify the delegation of competences to the Community. This Article states that if an action appears to be necessary for achieving one of the objectives of the Community, the Council may decide unanimously (after consultation with the European Parliament) to take appropriate measures. This Article has been used extensively to justify Community legislation in new areas (such as the environment prior to the Single European Act). The requirement of unanimity has also meant that the extension of competences has been guided by political opportunities rather than by any explicit economic or legal principles. However, Article 235 is capable of being a much more powerful instrument than this makes it sound: it is capable of providing the legal basis for directives that are stated in fairly general terms, but whose effect is to ensure that subsequent legislation necessary to achieve the objectives set in the directives can be passed by qualified majority.

The allocation of competences to the Community has also been confirmed by the Court of Justice. Member states have sometimes challenged proposed directives on the grounds that these involved extensions of Community competences. The Court in its rulings has often adopted a teleological approach to the interpretation of the Treaty of Rome (see Kovar, 1990); according to this approach, the competences of the Community are derived from the objectives of the Treaty. In particular, the Court has used the idea that the rules established by the Treaty imply the conditions under which these rules can be implemented. In other words, conditions that are deemed necessary *or* sufficient for the implementation of the Treaty are also covered by the Treaty.[2]

Implicitly, therefore, the Court has often found itself in the position of having to make judgments about the relative merits of Community action and action by the member states. It has appealed to a 'rule of reason'. The jurisprudence (see Vandersanden, 1992) regarding this rule of reason suggests that the concepts of efficiency and the common interest are the main justifications for Community legislation. The Court has also insisted that Community actions should be proportional to the importance of the matters at hand. And it has used a cumulative logic of integration (that is, its interpretation of what is required to fulfil the Treaty's objectives is related to the degree of European integration already achieved). For instance, it has established that if the Community has a competence in internal affairs (which suggests a degree of integration already attained), it will automatically have an analogous competence in external affairs.

Judicial review, then, is a mechanism for the confirmation of competences that involves substantive judgments on the relative merits of Community and member state action (via the teleological interpretation of the Treaty) *by an institution of the Community itself*. It contrasts therefore with the use of Article 235 which remains under the control of member states through their use of veto rights in the Council.

Competences can either be shared between the member states and the Community or exclusive to either party. Whenever the Community has a competence, the presumption is that it is shared. For instance, competences in agricultural and transport policies are shared, and in principle all competences that have been delegated under Article 235 are shared.

Shared competences are exercised in such a way that the Community has a right of pre-emption. Member states can use their competences as long as the Community has not exercised its own competence. Whenever the Community has exercised its competence, that of the member states is residual. Member states also have the obligation to respect Community law (there is primacy of Community law) and the spirit of Community action when they exercise their own competence.

Strictly speaking, competences that are exclusive to the Community arise only for matters in which the Community has the obligation to take action, and even then only when member states have been deprived formally of their own competences. Such situations are very rare; the Court has established them only for commercial policy and the protection of marine biological resources. Importantly, there are many areas where the Community has the obligation to take action but where the member states have not been formally deprived of their competence. These areas include the removal of barriers to the movement of goods, people, services and capital (Article 8A), commercial policy (Article 113), competition policy, the organization of agricultural markets, the preservation of the sea (Article 102) and transport policy. Cohesion (which involves a strengthening of social and regional policy) and the environment have been added by the Single European Act.

Competences that are exclusive to the member states are those that have not been delegated to the Community. Nevertheless, member states are supposed to respect the competences of the Community in the exercise of their own and to contribute to the achievement of its objectives.

2.2   The Instruments of Community Legislation and their Implementation

Under Article 189 of the Treaty of Rome, the Community has three types of instrument with which to exercise its competences: regulations, directives and decisions. *Regulations* are directly binding and addressed to member states.[3] These are used when precise provisions of implementation are required (for instance in commercial policy). *Directives* specify objectives to be reached by member states, which leave them to choose the appropriate form and method in their own legislation. *Decisions* are directly binding on those to whom they are addressed, and are used typically when the Commission has to rule on the legality of particular actions (for instance in competition policy)

In principle, the use of any instrument (whether a directive, a regulation or a decision) is subject to a decision in Council.[4] This means that the delegation of competences by member states to the Community is not intended as a blank cheque; member states can still exercise influence when particular pieces of legislation are proposed.

Until the Single European Act in 1986, unanimity was also required for most decisions of the Council (member states usually had a right of veto). This was due not so much to the terms of the original Treaty (which had provided that in certain areas such as agriculture unanimity would be replaced after a transitional period by qualified majority voting) as to the 'Luxembourg compromise' of 1966, which had ensured that *de facto* veto power was retained for all important decisions (with some notable exceptions such as the overruling of the United Kingdom on farm price increases in 1982, where the Council disagreed with the UK government's view that farm prices were a matter vital to its interests). In this context, individual member states could therefore have a decisive impact on Community legislation, both when delegation under Article 235 was required to establish competence and when particular texts were presented to the Council. The Single European Act has now introduced decisions by qualified majority in most areas of policy. Member states have therefore retained the ability to exercise a decisive influence through veto and the threat of veto only in matters for which competences have not yet been granted to the Community and in matters (like taxation) for which competence is established but the unanimity requirement has been kept. Interestingly, these matters do not include commercial policy: in spite of recent arguments between France and the rest of the Community, no member state has the power to veto Community participation in the Blair House agreement that has paved the way for a conclusion to the Uruguay Round of the GATT. Only the spirit of the Luxembourg compromise can be invoked in this matter.

The Council can also delegate its power of implementation to the Commission. This has been undertaken (through Regulation 17 in 1962) for competition policy. In this area, the Commission decides and its powers are subject only to non-binding advice from the competition policy authorities of the member states. Such delegation is exceptional and according to some commentators (Rosenthal, 1990), member states sometimes regret it.

In principle, Community laws are implemented by the member states. Accordingly, even if legislation has been subject to a progressive centralization in the Community, legislative implementation remains almost entirely decentralized.

2.3 Subsidiarity in the Treaty of Maastricht

The principle of subsidiarity was formally introduced into Community law[5] in the Treaty of Maastricht.[6] The relevant Article reads as follows:

'The Community shall act within the limits of the powers conferred upon it by this Treaty and of the objectives assigned to it therein.

'In areas which do not fall within its exclusive competence, the Community shall take action, in accordance with the principle of subsidiarity, only if and in so far as the objectives of the proposed action cannot be sufficiently achieved by the Member States and can therefore,

> by reason of the scale or effects of the proposed action, be better achieved by the Community.

> 'Any action by the Community shall not go beyond what is necessary to achieve the objectives of this Treaty.'

The wording of the second sentence of this Article reflects a difficult compromise between German and UK positions at the summit. The Germans proposed to define subsidiarity in terms of effectiveness, so that the Community should undertake actions which could be better achieved or attained at the supranational level. By contrast, the British insisted that Community actions should be undertaken only when this was necessary or essential for the achievement of the objective in question. Efficiency and necessity are different motivations and in principle neither implies the other. Some actions may be necessary to fulfil some objective of the Treaty (including some broad political objectives) without being efficient (if efficiency is assessed in terms of narrower economic criteria). Some actions may also be efficient without being strictly necessary. The final wording of the text includes both elements and seems to imply that if the objectives of an action cannot be fulfilled by the member states, Community intervention is expected to be more efficient.

In its public comment (AE 1804/5), the Commission has inverted this logic by suggesting that if an action is shown to be more efficient at the Community level, then the objectives of the action will be better fulfilled, so that action at the Community level is also necessary.

The last paragraph of the Article is often referred to as the principle of proportionality, according to which the Community should use instruments in proportion with the objectives at hand. This has been interpreted by the Commission as suggesting that it should use directives rather than regulations and that the degree of detail in directives should be reduced. Some member states have appealed to this principle recently to limit the Commission's involvement in the actual implementation of Community policies: for instance France, Germany and the UK dispute the Commission's role in the definition of priorities and the monitoring of disbursements in the implementation of regional policy in regions of industrial decline.

Nevertheless, the principle of proportionality is probably less controversial than the central paragraph of the Article. Controversies have already arisen regarding its interpretation, legal standing and implementation.

In its commentary (AE 1804/5), the Commission has expressed the view that the principle of subsidiarity does not affect the mechanisms through which competences can be allocated to the Community. In other words, according to the Commission, the principle does not conflict with the use of Article 235 or the teleological interpretation of the Treaty. The Commission takes the view that the principle merely regulates the way in which the shared competences are exercised.

In contrast, some public bodies in member states (the French Senate, for example) have taken the view that the Article significantly limits the actions of the Community. Rather than considering the objectives of the Treaty of Rome as a principle for allocating competences (with no explicit principle to regulate the manner in which they are exercised), the view of the Senate appears to be that it is the principle of subsidiarity that should govern the allocation of new competences, with the objectives of the Treaty regarded merely as a principle regulating their exercise. Under this interpretation, the principle of subsidiarity has been understood as the *sole* principle for the allocation of competences within the Community, which would considerably restrict the use of Article 235.

The wording of the principle is not explicit about the definition of exclusive competences. If a strict legalistic interpretation is followed (see Section 2.1 above), those competences will be limited to commercial policy and the protection of the sea. The Commission has, however, favoured (in AE 1804/5) a much broader interpretation, according to which the exclusive competences are those where the four freedoms (movement of goods, capital, services and people) are involved. The

Commission has therefore suggested that the removal of barriers to the movement of goods, capital, services and people (Article 8A), as well as policies that are corollary to the four freedoms, including commercial policy, competition policy, the organization of agricultural markets, the protection of the sea, and transport policy (a large block of Community actions!) belong to the sphere of exclusive competence and accordingly are not subject to the principle of subsidiarity. They are nevertheless accepted to be subject to the principle of proportionality.[7]

It seems fair to conclude that the principle of subsidiarity remains, as it stands, very general and open to many interpretations. The authors of the Maastricht Treaty did not clearly establish the principle as an instrument for the allocation as well as the exercise of competences, and they chose not to give a list of particular areas where Community action was likely to be necessary and efficient. They did not put forward any guidelines for judging the effectiveness and necessity of a particular action. The principle of subsidiarity at the level of the Community therefore remains a general political principle rather than a source of explicit guidance. The political philosophy that it expresses (namely that centralization should be undertaken only when a good case can be made for it) is unexceptionable.[8] But without further clarification, it is hard to implement in practice.

Implementation of the principle of subsidiarity will *de facto* be the responsibility of the European Court of Justice, specifically when it takes action under Article 173 to review the legality of Community actions. Quite apart from the potential increase in its workload, the absence of even broad guidelines in the Maastricht Treaty means the Court may have been assigned a task beyond its capacity. Indeed, the Court is supposed to rule only on the legality of actions and not to judge their effectiveness in some broader sense. There is a risk that, in straying into very obviously political territory, the Court may jeopardize its hard-won credibility.[9]

The Birmingham declaration of the Council of Ministers implicitly recognized the shortcomings of leaving implementation to the Court of Justice, and it called for the definition of 'subsidiarity tests' to be applied by the Council at the stage of preparing legislation. The procedure for implementing these subsidiarity tests, which remain rather vague, was agreed at the Edinburgh summit, with the important provision that they require only a qualified majority in the Council.

Considering the implementation problem therefore only reinforces the conclusion that the European Community lacks an explicit procedure for the allocation of competences and that the principle of subsidiarity needs to be further clarified. It is the purpose of this Report to see how far economic analysis can contribute to the clarification of the principle. First, though, we summarize briefly the extent to which, notwithstanding the vagueness of the underlying principles, Community powers have developed relative to those of member states, and we compare them in broad terms to those exercised in federal states.

2.4 The Nature of Community Power

2.4.1 The F-Word or the C-Word?: The Meaning of Majority Vote

We described in Section 2.2 above the way in which the Single European Act had brought about a transition in practice from unanimity to qualified majority voting in many areas of policy decision-making in the Community. What this means is that, regardless of current arguments between pro- and anti-federalists about the *future* of Europe, the Community is already a federation in the most essential sense of that term. However, it continues to operate with many of the institutions, and with the lack of structural clarity, of a confederation.

The difference between a federation and a confederation has been the subject of long and often inconclusive arguments. For our purposes, the critical distinction lies in the degree of sovereignty of the members. In a confederation, the central authority cannot impose decisions on any of its members, since each member has veto power. Indeed, in an important sense there *is* no central authority, merely a mechanism for coordinating the decisions of independent members. In a federation, by contrast, central decisions do not need to be unanimous. If an appropriate majority of members votes in favour of a measure, this becomes binding on all.

The EC clearly began as a confederation, initially focused on a very limited set of issues (coal and steel), with a decision process requiring unanimity. Over the last 35 years, the scope of the EC has grown immensely, and the set of issues under its competence has become wide-ranging. This gradual growth of Community involvement did not acquire a centralized character, however, until the Single European Act changed the rules whereby decisions are reached. With this change, the EC acquired a clear federal identity. But while its nature changed, the Community's institutions were not adapted to take this evolution into account. In particular, no clear separation was introduced between national and central authority. The government of the Community – the Council of Ministers – is the assembly of the ministers of the national governments of the member states. On the other hand, the European Parliament, a federal institution in spirit, was never given any substantial power. The EC is operating as a federation but working with the institutions of a confederation.

2.4.2 The Main Policy Areas

The importance of Community activities relative to those of the member states is often assessed in terms of the relative budgetary resources deployed. By this criterion the EC is extremely decentralized: total Community disbursements (at 60 billion ECU in 1992) are similar to those of Denmark. The resources of the Community include taxes on the production of sugar and agricultural products, import duties, and a value added tax of 1.4% applied to a common basis across states. Proceeds from VAT represent by far the largest source of income for the Community. Overall, member states contribute less than 1% of their GDP to the Community budget (with the exceptions of the Benelux, Greece and Portugal). As far as expenditures are concerned, the cost of operating Community institutions amounts to only 5% of the budget. The Common Agricultural Policy absorbs about 60%, and it is more than five times as expensive as regional policy. The Community has to balance its income and expenditure. Borrowing is allowed only for helping member states facing balance-of-payments difficulties (up to a maximum of 14 billion ECU) and to help finance investments together with the European Investment Bank (up to a total of 3.75 billion ECU).

Nevertheless, budgetary indicators are a poor criterion of the degree of central authority, for two main reasons. First, in a number of areas the disbursements of member states are constrained by Community laws. Second, in many areas Community competences focus on matters that are managed by rule-making and require little in the way of budgetary disbursements. In what follows we examine these areas case by case.

Internal Trade and Factor Movements. The Community has widespread competences in this area, derived from the Treaty of Rome and reinforced by the Single European Act. In the last few years it has passed a large number of directives (about 300) as part of the single-market programme. Goods, services and capital movements throughout the Community, in particular, have been subject to significant liberalization.

Taxation. As we have indicated, the Community has very little power to tax (its main resource being a surcharge on VAT). Nevertheless, the Community has competence (following Articles 95–99 of the Treaty of Rome) regarding the harmonization of indirect taxes. Significant harmonization has been achieved since 1985. The Community has tried to establish a competence concerning direct taxes (on individuals and companies) on the basis of Article 100 of the Treaty (which requires unanimity). In this area, the Community favours negotiation between member states rather than harmonization.

Industrial and R&D Policy. Outside the coal and steel industries, the Community has few competences relating directly to industrial policy. Its competences are based either on the articles related to competition policy or those relating to the internal market. Accordingly, an industrial policy in the Community is always justified as a necessary part of competition policy or as a necessary ingredient of the internal market. Community policies are most active for telecommunications, energy and utilities.

The competences of the Community with respect to R&D are nevertheless widespread (Article 130 of the Single European Act). One of the explicit objectives of its policy in the area is to avoid duplication in research and to organize coordination among member states. At the end of the 1980s, the EC budget for R&D represented about 4% of total disbursements by member states in this field. Only in the area of energy policy are Community expenditures significantly greater (about 15% of those by member states).

Competition Policy. Competences for competition policy stem directly from Articles 85–94 of the Treaty and from a Council regulation (justified on the basis of Article 235) regarding the control of concentrations (the 'Merger Regulation'). In the area of competition policy, the allocation of competences between the Community and the member states is fairly clear: competences of the member states under the treaty are limited to operations which do not affect intra-EC trade. In the area of concentrations, competences are allocated by a rule which attempts to take into account the spillovers of proposed operations across states (see our discussion in Chapter 7 below). Competition policy is therefore rather unusual: it is the one area where the allocation of competence has been formalized. In addition, as we have indicated, it is an area where the powers of the Council have been delegated to the Commission.

Regional Policy and the Social Fund. Competences for regional policy have been formalized by the Single European Act, which modified the Treaty of Rome by emphasizing cohesion as an objective of the Treaty (Articles 130A and 130C). Between 1975 and 1989, some 27 billion ECU were spent under this heading. Such amounts were small relative to GDP and small relative to member states' own expenditures on regional development, except for those of Portugal, but the total amount spent per year on regional development has increased markedly since 1989. The total budget for 1993 amounts to 14 billion ECU. This year, Greece and Ireland are due to receive as much as 3% of their GDP in financial assistance (outside the European Agricultural Guarantee and Guidance Fund [EAGGF] and the social funds) and Portugal as much as 3.7%. The Treaty of Rome (in Articles 123–8) also established the Social Fund, with the objective of encouraging employment, and in particular reducing unemployment among the young and those unemployed for more than a year. Its main action is the co-financing of education and training, for a total of about 4 billion ECU in 1990. Since the reform of the structural funds in 1989, actions under the regional and social funds and those of the EAGGF (at least in respect of the guidance component) are supposed to be integrated.

Agriculture. Competence in agriculture stems directly from the Treaty (Article 39). The main instruments of the policy are the support of prices and structural programmes. Since 1988, resources have been shifted within the fund (EAGGF) from price support to guidance. Member states have kept widespread competences in this area.

Environment. The original Treaty does not give competence to the Community in this area. Accordingly, Article 235 has been used in order to allocate some competences. These were explicitly recognized in the Single European Act (Article 130), which also adopted a number of principles (like the 'polluter pays' principle) to be followed in Community policy. Important directives which leave little room for national discretion have been put forward in the area of atmospheric pollution, dangerous chemicals and water pollution, and also regarding the protection of flora and fauna (including restrictions on the killing of baby seals), noise emissions, experiments on animals and so on. The Community has also encouraged international agreements like the conventions on the Rhine, the Baltic and the Mediterrannean.

Commercial Policy. The Community has extensive competence under the Treaty of Rome (Articles 110–16) to establish a common commercial policy and in particular to conclude tariff agreements. It is one of the two areas where the Community has been formally granted exclusive competence. The Community has negotiated numerous bilateral and multilateral agreements (with the US, Japan, EFTA and so on) and has established a common system of tariffs (the Common External Tariff).

Transport. The Treaty of Rome is explicit about the obligation for the Community to determine a common transport policy (Articles 74–75). There are, however, no guiding principles. The Community has passed directives about entry conditions and prices in the road transport industry. Air transport has become an area of competence since the Single European Act and decisions by the Court of Justice that competition policy applies to this sector. Some liberalization of the sector has since been implemented.

Monetary Policy. Monetary integration was not an objective of the Treaty (and hence could not give rise to competence) until the Single European Act (Article 102A). Formally, the European Monetary System is an agreement between the central banks and not strictly a Community policy. In this area, the Community acts only as a broker in multilateral negotiations. Competences for the European monetary union are specified by the Treaty of Maastricht.

Social Policy. The Community has some competence arising from Articles 48–51 for policies towards migrant workers of EC origin, and it has adopted a number of directives to facilitate the movement of workers (including, importantly, the coordination of social security rights for migrant workers). It has also acquired some competence (through Article 235) for the training of handicapped workers. The Single European Act has also given some competence for the organization of a social dialogue and for health and safety at work (Articles 100A and 118A). A large number of directives which harmonize conditions for health and safety have been put forward since 1985.

2.5 A Comparison with Existing Federations

2.5.1 The Allocation of Functions

Pommerehne (1977) provides an explicit comparison of the functions performed by central, state and local governments in the United States, Canada, Germany and Switzerland. He concludes that the allocation of functions between levels of governments is very similar in those four

Table 2.1: Division of Responsibilities Between Central and Local Governments for European Community and Other Typical Federations.

	Typical Federations	*European Community*
National defence	F	S
International relations	F	F/S
Broadcasting systems	F	F/S
Social insurance	F	S
Agriculture (price stabilization and income)	F	F
Monetary policy	F	M
Commercial policy	F	F/S
Air transport	F	F/S
Competition policy	F/S	F/S
Universities and basic research	F/S	F/S
Environmental protection	F/S	F/S
Secondary education	S	S
Health and hospitals	S	S
Public utilities	S	S
Transport (excluding rail/postal services)	S	S
Retirement schemes	S	S
Law enforcement	S	S

Note: F (S) denotes a function performed at the federal (state) level; F/S denotes a function shared by federal and state levels; M refers to functions that will be performed at the federal level if the objectives of the Maastricht Treaty are fully implemented.

federations. Table 2.1 compares the typical allocation of power that he reports with that observed in the Community, as we have described it above. Since the allocation of power between national and local governments varies a great deal across member states of the Community, the comparison is undertaken only for the allocation between federal and state governments, comparing this with the allocation between the EC and its member states.

Table 2.1 concentrates on where the main balance of power lies, so that (for instance) the judgement that law enforcement is typically a state responsibility is not invalidated by the existence of the FBI or the Royal Canadian Mounted Police. It is important, nevertheless, to note that it is much harder to reach appropriate judgements about where power lies in the European Community than in typical federations, which is reflected in the greater proportion of EC functions reported as shared. This underlines once again the lack of clarity in the European allocation of powers and functions compared to those in explicitly federal states.

The comparison in Table 2.1 is in one respect rather striking. It suggests that the European Community already shares with its member states many of the functions that are typically performed by a federation (though it may carry out these functions in very different ways). It is only in the areas of defence, international relations and social insurance that the Community lacks competence relative to typical federations. Importantly, it does not appear to have gained any competences other than those enjoyed by typical federal authorities.

Federations do differ a great deal in the degree of power enjoyed by state and federal authorities in taxation matters. In contrast to Germany, the Swiss constitution grants little power to the centre to raise taxes (the US is in a intermediate position). The European Community is in a position similar to that of the federal level in Switzerland, with a surcharge on indirect taxes as the prime source of income and little freedom to raise additional taxes.

Pommerehne (1990) argues that fiscal decentralization is a key feature of the control exercised by lower jurisdictions on the federal level in Switzerland and has played a major role in containing the growth of public expenditures. The Swiss experience also indicates that a modest budget at the centre is sufficient to undertake many of the functions usually allocated to the federal level. This includes social insurance, though as we discuss in Chapter 4 the degree of social insurance carried out at the federal level (as opposed to the cantonal level) in Switzerland is modest compared to that in other countries.

2.5.2 The Nature of Federal Institutions

There are two important features of federal states that are missing today in the Community: first, a relatively clear separation between central and state governments; and second, a well-defined process through which the allocation of power between central and local authority can be altered. In the historical development of today's existing federations, these features have arisen out of the concern to balance two conflicting considerations: the need to give voice to the interest of the majority of individuals living in the federation, and the need to protect the national interests of the member states. The balance between these two requirements has typically been achieved through the creation of four kinds of federal institution:

(a)   A federal parliament, whose members are elected in proportion to population. This institution is designed to give weight to majority will.

(b)   A federal upper house, where each member state has the same number of members. This institution is meant to give equal standing to all member states, independent of their size.

(c)   A federal government, truly supranational and not an extension of the participating national governments.

(d)   A federal supreme court.

Table 2.2 illustrates the details of these institutions for a number of federations. The institutional design of the EC, while clearly inspired by this model, differs from it in many important ways. In particular, the balance between majority will and minority interest is achieved not by checks and balances among institutions each of which has a clear set of interests to represent, but by a kind of compromise in the make-up of

Table 2.2: Institutional Structure of Federations.

Country	Lower House	Upper House	Federal Government	Federal Court
Australia	House of Representatives	Senate (10 members for each state)	Prime Minister and Cabinet	Federal Court
Canada	House of Commons	Senate (unequal weight to each state, from 4 to 24 members)	Prime Minister and Cabinet	Supreme Court
Germany	Federal Chamber (Bundestag)	Federal Council (Bundesrat) (unequal weight to each state, from 2 to 5 members)	Chancellor (Bundeskanzler) and Cabinet	Federal Constitutional Tribunal (Bundesverfassungsgericht)
Switzerland	National Council	Council of States (2 members for each canton)	Federal Council	Federal Tribunal
USA	House of Representatives	Senate (2 members for each state)	President and Cabinet	Supreme Court

individual institutions. Thus the Council of Ministers (the 'European government'), for example, is the union of national governments, so that all members have a voice, but the Council votes according to a particular rule (qualified majority) that gives greater weight to larger countries. Similarly, the members of the European Commission are allocated on the basis of nationality, again with larger states having the right to more Commissioners. The number of members of the European Parliament depends on the size of the population of each member state, but small countries are given a more than proportional share of representatives (and an analogous principle determines the votes exercised in Council by each member state).

It is important to note that this kind of compromise is not just another way to achieve what federal institutions do. In particular, it has a tendency to make smaller countries more influential in all matters than they would be under exactly proportional weighting. It makes no distinction between ordinary matters, however, and those in which important interests are at stake, which motivates the use of different institutions (such as a Senate and a House of Representatives) to act as checks upon one another. The functioning of the EC compromise is also dependent on the exact arithmetic of the voting procedure: under the present system, the EC's five large countries need the support of at least two small states to reach a qualified majority, and the seven small states need to persuade at least three of the large ones. With the probable admission of Austria, Finland, Norway and Sweden in 1995, however, the smaller countries will become proportionately more powerful. If they voted as a bloc, eleven countries with a combined population slightly below that of Germany would exercise nearly half of all the votes in Council, thus transforming a device intended to protect minority rights into a dominant determinant of everyday decisions.[10]

Recent debates over the principle of subsidiarity reflect an anxiety on the part of many in the Community that present and future trends in the evolution of power may not give adequate weight to the interests of nation states and other groups that find themselves out of sympathy with majority opinion. It is ironic, therefore, that this anxiety should manifest itself as a fear of federalism. The Community is already essentially federal, but it appears to have acquired this character in a fit of absence of mind. It possesses neither the institutions nor the procedures that would permit the centralizing potential inherent in majority voting to be tempered by a systematic attention to minority concerns. In what follows we shall be concerned with one particular aspect of this issue, namely the potential for developing subsidiarity as a clear and practical principle for the allocation and the exercise of powers. It is all the more important to do so given the important shortcomings of the other procedures and institutions of the present Community.

Notes

[1] In addition, all Community decisions require a legal basis (Article 190).

[2] Some legal commentators (see Vandersanden 1992) have said that the competences of the Community are 'virtual' and have to be revealed by the Court.

[3] Legislation can sometimes be addressed, however, to moral or physical persons distinct from member states, but disguised as a regulation.

[4] In the context of Article 90, however, which deals with public undertakings, decisions can be taken without Council's approval.

[5] The principle of subsidiarity is already present, at least informally, in the ECSC and EURATOM treaties.

[6] Formally, this is Article G of the treaty on the European Union, which modifies the Treaty of Rome by adding on Article 3b.

[7] Douglas Hurd, the UK Foreign Minister, has said that he insisted that the last sentence in Article 3b be detached from the previous paragraph, thereby ensuring that the principle apply to all Community actions (see Duff, 1993, p. 9).

[8] The idea of subsidiarity is central to Christian moral philosophy. It was developed by Althusius (a Calvinist) in the sixteenth century and adopted by the Catholic church in Pope Pius XI's encyclical *Quadragesimo Anno* (1931). It has affinities to elements in the political philosophy of various authors in the nineteenth century (such as Proudhon and John Stuart Mill).

[9] This should not be exaggerated, however; as we have indicated, in developing a rule of reason, the Court has already been making such substantive judgments.

[10] See 'The maths of post-Maastricht Europe', *The Economist*, 16 October 1993, pp. 45-6.

3 The Principles of Subsidiarity

We emphasized in Chapter 1 that subsidiarity is not the same thing as decentralization. Any realistic allocation of political and economic powers will be a compromise between the claims of decentralization and those of centralization; subsidiarity is the specific claim that the burden of proof in the process of making this trade-off should lie in favour of decentralization. Nevertheless, we can begin a systematic examination of the principle of subsidiarity only by analysing the strengths and weaknesses of centralized and decentralized forms of government. Where do their respective comparative advantages lie?

These strengths and weaknesses will be evaluated in terms of three main kinds of consideration: *efficiency* in the allocation of resources; *equity* or fairness in their distribution; and *accountability* of the agencies of the state to the people in whose name they are granted power. Most economic analysis makes frequent reference to the first two considerations, often taking it for granted that once problems with efficiency and equity have been identified, policies can be designed to remedy them. In recent years, however, there has been increasing concern with problems of 'government failure', which can often be more serious than the market failure to which government action is a response. Economic analysis has increasingly had to take into account the need to make government and its agencies accountable, and many of the most powerful arguments deployed in the debate over subsidiarity concern its impact on accountability. Even if, as we believe, accountability is often desirable precisely because it enhances efficiency, equity or both, it will be helpful to pay explicit attention to the value of accountability in the analysis that follows.

3.1 The Benefits of Centralization

3.1.1 Efficiency

In principle both centralized and decentralized forms of government could end up implementing rather similar policies, but there are a number of circumstances in which there is good reason to expect centralized government to lead to greater efficiency. We distinguish three:

Spillovers. Policies implemented in one locality may have effects on the welfare of the population in another locality. For instance, the provision of secondary education by one locality may have a beneficial effect (via labour mobility) on another, which the former has no incentive to take into account when determining its level of provision. Or one locality may regulate airborne pollution (such as acid rain) relatively mildly because most of the cost is borne by other localities downwind. Spillovers may often affect several interest groups in the economies concerned: for example, countries setting product standards that are incompatible with those of other countries may do so intentionally to put foreign producers at a competitive disadvantage; they may also thereby add to the confusion and uncertainty faced by consumers (foreign and domestic) which was the rationale for setting product standards in the first place.

Economies of Scale. Some public goods (such as defence) cost much less if provided by a single jurisdiction rather than by several separate ones. Others (such as systems of regulation, or educational curricula) may be of better quality if provided centrally. Some of the most important sources of economies of scale are informational, as in the provision of research and development. Others arise from an increased ability to coordinate (as in the integration of armies under single chains of command). Only some are traditional scale economies arising from costs that decline with larger production runs.

Insurance. To the extent that different localities are exposed to macroeconomic shocks that are less than perfectly correlated, there is scope for pooling of risks among them. This pooling may be more easily achieved by means of transfers within a single jurisdiction in response to shocks than by transfers among independent localities, since there is unlikely to be a market for macroeconomic insurance.

3.1.2 Equity

We distinguish two advantages of centralization in terms of equity:

Redistribution within Localities. If localities attempt redistributive taxation, they may be frustrated by the mobility of the poorest and the richest of their citizens – the former towards and the latter away from the most redistributive localities. Redistribution by a central authority (that is, one covering an area beyond which the population is relatively immobile) faces no such difficulty.

Redistribution among Localities. It is usually observed that the willingness of states to make redistributive transfers within their own borders is considerably greater than their willingness to make transfers to localities which may be equally deserving but lie outside their borders. Consequently, we should expect centralization to increase the extent of transfers among localities, since it increases the ability of the localities that would be beneficiaries of such redistribution to put the transfers into effect.

3.1.3 Accountability

Visibility. Centralization may help voters to monitor the actions of government by increasing the visibility of its actions. The extent to which this is true will depend, of course, on a number of features of the political culture of the jurisdiction concerned: a common language, a press concerned with central rather than purely regional issues, and political parties that organize throughout the jurisdiction, rather than being regionally based, will all enhance the visibility of centralized policies. These are features of some European countries (France, for example) which are strikingly absent from others (such as Switzerland).

3.1.4 Coordination or Centralization?

All these six advantages of centralization appeal to the fact that the policies of localities may produce better results if they are coordinated rather than undertaken independently. This raises the question why it is necessary to centralize power to achieve coordination: why can the necessary coordination not be achieved by agreements among independent localities? For instance, localities could agree to provide higher levels of secondary education or regulate pollution more stringently than they would have done independently; they could cooperate to share the costs of common defence; they could write insurance contracts specifying transfers between them contingent on the kind of macroeconomic shock they face (e.g. the price of oil); and they could agree levels of progressivity of their tax systems and levels of transfers between regions. Such agreements might, for a variety of reasons, be difficult to implement or monitor, and localities would all have an incentive to 'cheat' while hoping that other localities would keep their side of the bargain. The advantage of centralization would then consist in the extent to which it provides a more *credible* mechanism for achieving such coordination than these agreements would on their own.

The difference between coordination of policies and centralization of power lies in the fact that under coordination, localities retain the right to determine policies as they wish, subject to negotiation with other localities; under centralization, they can be overruled. This corresponds, then, to the distinction we introduced in Chapter 2 between *confederation* and *federation*. We argued there that the EC has already taken (in the Single European Act) significant steps towards federation – that is, to centralization. And our discussion in this chapter has led us to argue that centralization is likely to be desirable in the presence of two simultaneous failures of decentralization: first, that non-cooperative policy-making yields results that are significantly worse than cooperative policy-making; and second, agreements to cooperate without centralizing are not very credible. Their credibility will depend on how easily the parties can observe whether or not they are being kept, on the effectiveness of any sanctions they can impose on each other when they are broken, and on how great the temptation is for countries to 'cheat'. So, for example, we would expect centralization to be more desirable the greater the number of parties who have to monitor each others' cooperation, and the more imprecise the nature of the policy on which they seek to agree. We shall illustrate these points in the particular areas of policy we discuss in the remaining chapters of the Report.

Sometimes the reason why cooperation is hard is not so much the difficulty of enforcing cooperative agreements as the difficulty of reaching them in the first place. This will be particularly true where there are a number of possible alternative cooperative policies, all more efficient than the existing non-cooperative policies but with different implications for the distribution of gains and losses between parties. For example, the setting of product standards is designed to alleviate the market failures resulting from consumers' lack of information about product quality. The decision over which and how many standards to set is a compromise between consumers' preferences for variety (which implies that more standards are desirable) and economies of scale, which may be either technical (as in the case of standards for telecommunications equipment) or related to the difficulty of having adequate information to choose from more than a small number of alternative product specifications. If countries set incompatible product standards, markets will be inefficiently fragmented, but if the number of standards is reduced, there will be a competitive advantage enjoyed by the producers who have been used to manufacturing to those standards that are retained (see Gatsios and Seabright, 1989). The difficulty of reaching agreement over harmonization of product standards led the EC in 1985 to opt for the less demanding policy of 'mutual recognition'. While undoubtedly an improvement on the status quo, this may have left the Community with an inefficiently large number of alternative standards jostling for consumers' attention. The establishment of a centralized body to set standards without the explicit agreement of member states on each occasion might have been a preferable solution, provided member states could trust such a body not to be biased towards the interests of producers in any particular member state.

3.2 The Advantages of Decentralization

What, in contrast, are the advantages of decentralization? These lie in the domain of efficiency and accountability, since typically decentralization makes it harder to pursue concerns about equity (in the sense of distributive justice).[1]

3.2.1 Efficiency

Under the heading of efficiency we distinguish four circumstances favouring decentralization:

Uncertainty about Local Conditions. Central authorities may be less well informed than local ones about practical conditions affecting the local implementation of policies (where bus-stops should be located, the nature of agroclimatic conditions, and so on).

Uncertainty about Local Preferences. Central authorities may be in less close touch than local ones with the wishes of local people (for instance, about their preferences as between improved transport and protection of the countryside, or labour regulation and the promotion of employment, or between high product standards and low-cost products).

Uncertainty about the Effects of New Policies. When the designers of a policy have little information about its likely effects, allowing localities to experiment and comparing the results may provide valuable information that can be used in future policy design. There may still be less experimentation than would be ideal, since localities will not take into account the informational benefit they create for other localities (to put it another way, localities will be reluctant to become guinea-pigs). This may nevertheless be preferable to the relatively uniform policies likely to be adopted by central authorities.

Regional Differentiation of Policies. Even when central authorities are no less well informed, centrally-determined policies may be less flexible and responsive to local conditions, either because of rules of equal treatment across localities or because central authorities prefer simple and relatively uniform policies. For example, income tax rates, when determined centrally, are typically uniform for the country as a whole.

3.2.2 Accountability

Decentralization allows the citizens of a locality to express their dissatisfaction with their government if it does not implement the policies they wish. They may do this in two ways:

Citizens' Mobility. Citizens dissatisfied with their government can move to another jurisdiction whose policies they prefer. The fear of losing taxpayers will act as an incentive for local governments to use resources efficiently and provide levels and kinds of public goods that reflect taxpayers' preferences. In effect, local jurisdictions can be thought of as 'firms' supplying differentiated products whose different characteristics correspond to the various public goods and services provided in a locality. The extreme version of this argument is Tiebout's (1956) hypothesis, named after the economist who proposed that competition between jurisdictions would lead to an efficient allocation of resources even in the presence of public goods. The precise conditions under which this will occur are extremely restrictive (see Appendix 3.1). However, the hypothesis encapsulates a potentially important insight. Governments can use the fact that the consumption of many public goods is dependent upon location to help solve the problem of inducing voters to reveal their true preferences for levels of public good provision, since voters who claim not to want certain public goods can be excluded from nevertheless consuming them once they are provided. Although we shall discuss in Chapter 4 some significant costs of voter mobility, the Tiebout insight is that it may also have benefits by helping to sort the population according to the varying kinds of preference for combinations of public goods.

There is also an important dynamic aspect to this which we discussed in Chapter 1. The ability of voters to move prevents a government which has induced them to reveal their preferences and other characteristics from subsequently exploiting this information to their disadvantage: it will have to offer them goods and services attractive enough to make them want to stay. This can be expected to make them more willing to reveal these characteristics.

Voting. Decentralization allows voters in a locality to decide collectively to replace their government if they are dissatisfied with its performance. If this mechanism of accountability works reasonably well (which itself depends on voters' preferences being sufficiently homogeneous for the electoral mechanism to represent them properly), centralization can only diminish its effectiveness. This is because centralization limits the power of the citizens of the locality to replace the government, since that decision will now depend also on the views of the citizens of other localities, who may feel differently about the government's performance.

3.2.3 Differentiation or Decentralization?

The four efficiency-based advantages of decentralization all appeal to the fact that it may be desirable to implement different policies for different localities. In Chapter 1, however, we pointed out that regional differentiation is not the same thing as decentralization. Again, this raises the question: why cannot a centralized government also differentiate its policies by locality? We may in practice observe that centralized policies tend to be relatively uniform, but why should this always be so? A central authority can have its employees based in the localities to inform it of local conditions; it can conduct its own local referenda and opinion polls (as the British government did, for example, in different counties of Wales over the proposals to relax the laws on licensing of alcohol consumption); it can implement policies of regional grants and subsidies; it can run pilot projects in some localities and not in others. A central government would surely do all of these things, if it were fully responsive to the diversity of citizens' preferences and could commit itself not to use the information supplied by its citizens (for example, about their tax-paying capacity) to their future disadvantage. Indeed, the main insight of the Tiebout hypothesis is available no less to a central government than to local ones: by differentiating its policies it can sort its population by location and therefore implicitly by preferences for public goods. It has no need to decentralize *government* in order to exploit this insight, and if it is already fully sensitive to the needs and interests of all its citizens, decentralization will bring them no further benefit.

Centralized policies are often in practice less regionally differentiated than decentralized policies would be, however, which must therefore be due to the fact that a centralized authority is *less* likely to be responsive to the welfare of all its citizens,[2] or cannot commit itself not to exploit the information they supply to their future disadvantage. In other words, it is less *accountable* than decentralized authorities; so the accountability advantages of decentralization are, from this perspective, the most fundamental. Central authorities *could*, in principle, differentiate their policies by locality to reflect the different conditions and preferences of those localities; but they are less likely to fear the reaction of dissatisfied citizens in any given locality if they do not do so, and less able to promise them credibly not to use the information they reveal in ways they would regret. The logic of the argument here parallels what we said above about centralization making cooperation more credible; here it is decentralization that increases the credibility of the state's commitment to local differentiation of policies.

This in turn implies that the loss of accountability entailed by centralization will be greatest when there is a low or negative correlation between the unexpected shocks to the welfare of different localities. Appendix 3.2 explores a simple model of centralization and accountability that makes this relationship more precise. To put it another way, what weakens local accountability is not in itself the risk that regions will require different policies; it is the risk that regions will be differentially satisfied with whatever policies they have.

3.2.4 The Effects of Diminished Accountability

The claim that centralization may lead to failures of accountability tells us nothing by itself about the kinds of distortion in public policy that may occur as a result. These will depend upon the way in which those individuals in charge of implementing public policy react to their freedom from accountability; it will therefore be a function of ' ~th their own personal interests and preferences and the interests of those outside pressure groups that can exert influence upon them. What has been called the phenomenon of 'regulatory capture' is the outcome of this process of pressure and influence (see Stigler, 1971; Laffont and Tirole, 1993, Chapter 11; Neven, Nuttall and Seabright, 1993, Chapter 6). This may tend towards interest group capture or bureaucratic capture according to the degree to which the outside pressures or the internal preferences of bureaucrats are dominant in determining the character of the policies pursued.

There is nevertheless one very influential hypothesis about government failure, which is sometimes known as the 'Leviathan' hypothesis (see Brennan and Buchanan, 1980) and is best seen as a special case of the phenomenon of regulatory capture. This claims that the interests of bureaucrats are always advanced by an increase in the budgets they command and the level of activity they undertake.[3] Consequently public policy will tend to be distorted (relative to the social optimum) in the direction of excessive taxing and spending – and, more generally, of excessive intervention in the economy. On this view, competition among jurisdictions provides taxpayers with a valuable escape option that makes it harder for Leviathans to exploit them. And the Leviathan view predicts that such competition should always lead to lower levels of taxation, expenditure and overall government activity than would otherwise occur. Whether this is generally true is an empirical matter which we consider below, but clearly it is not the only form of regulatory capture that can be envisaged. For example, if the state is unduly influenced by interest groups with a preference for relatively low levels of provision of public goods, then the interest of bureaucrats in large budgets will be outweighed by their desire to please those interest groups, and taxation and expenditure will be too low relative to the social optimum. The merits of competition between jurisdictions will then depend on whether mobility of the under-represented interest groups – their right of 'exit', to use Hirschman's (1970) phrase – increases sufficiently to compensate for their lack of 'voice'. It may on the contrary happen that the already influential groups become even more influential once their mobility is increased, a possibility we discuss in relation to competition policy in Chapter 7 below.

3.3 Which Powers Should Go Together?

In addition to the general merits of centralization and decentralization, we can also consider a third set of arguments: namely, factors that determine if certain policies should or should not be handled by the same level of jurisdiction, whether this is a central or a local one. We can call these economies and diseconomies of *scope* in policy-making. When there are economies of scope this will strengthen the case for policies' being assigned to the same level of government; when there are diseconomies of scope it will strengthen the case for assigning them to different levels.

3.3.1 Diseconomies of Scope

The most basic diseconomy of scope is diminished accountability. The greater the number of policies for which a given government is responsible, the harder it is for citizens to change a particular policy with which they disagree, since governments win or lose elections on the basis of whole packages of policies. It follows from this that the diseconomy of scope will be most serious between policies of very different kinds; that is, policies about which different citizens are likely to have different views of the government's performance. For instance, if voters think the government regulates the electricity industry well they will probably think it regulates the gas industry well; but this may bear very little relation to whether or not they approve of its policies on (say) education or public support for the arts.

3.3.2 Economies of Scope: Efficiency

Economies of scope can be of several kinds, of which we distinguish four, two related to efficiency and two to accountability:

Informational Economies. Certain kinds of policy-making require information and expertise that can be shared between policies (gas and electricity regulation is an example).

Coordination Economies. Certain policies require rapid coordination. For example, the allocation of responsibilities for transportation within a country is usually done by mode of transportation. This seems to neglect the fundamental nature of the good. From the point of view of consumers, a plane journey between Paris and Lyon is a closer substitute for a train journey between the two cities than for a plane journey between Paris and Toulouse. Yet it is the two plane journeys that are the responsibility of the same agency, not the two trips between Paris and Lyon. Why is that? In the day-to-day management of the transport system, the decisions to be taken are decisions that involve the planes and the crews that will fly between all towns. Very few short-run decisions involve planes and trains at the same time. It is true that for planning purposes one should weigh carefully the options of plane and train transport against each other. These decisions are made in circumstances where time is not a critical factor, and hence the extra difficulty of coordination between agencies is not very important.

3.3.3 Economies of Scope: Accountability

Voter observability. Citizens cannot be expected to participate in the monitoring and election of very many different layers of government; they therefore need to focus their attention on a limited number of layers, and policies need to be 'bundled' appropriately.

Cost Accountability. Levels of government empowered to make spending decisions should, in principle, also take the taxing decisions required to finance that spending, except in so far as the spending involves spillovers or explicit transfers between jurisdictions.

3.4 Accountability and Subsidiarity: The Evidence

We can summarize the message of our examination of the merits of centralization and decentralization as follows: centralization should in principle increase the credibility of cooperation between localities, and decentralization should increase the credibility of the accountability of the state to the needs of localities. On the face of it, there is no reason why either of these desiderata should take precedence over the other. The principle of subsidiarity claims, however, that when in doubt, decentralization should be preferred. It can therefore be interpreted as the expression of an essentially political judgement that good government is more likely to be under threat from failures of accountability than from failures of cooperation, and moreover that the kinds of distortion induced by these failures in accountability are of the kind that decentralization can help to alleviate (such as those described in the Leviathan hypothesis).

Though a political judgement, this is also an empirical judgement whose accuracy may vary from time to time and from place to place. Once we take seriously the fact that governments are not disinterested agents of the public good, judgements about the strengths and weaknesses of centralization and decentralization have to take into account the actual merits of the mechanisms of accountability at the different levels. For instance, if local political mechanisms persistently ignore the interests of certain groups, some of the obstacles to central accountability may paradoxically be beneficial: the ignored groups may have a national political weight even if they are too thinly spread to have local influence.[4] (Nevertheless, we should expect, other things equal, that centralization will usually tend to weaken accountability overall.) Likewise, whether or not control over particular policies should be decentralized will depend not just on the nature of the policies themselves, but also on the quality of the existing mechanisms of public choice at the local level. This may in turn depend on what other policies are decentralized, since local power may itself encourage active local participation and involvement in public affairs. For example, Table 3.1 shows that turnout in communal elections in Switzerland is significantly higher than in cantonal and national elections, whereas in the UK (a much more centralized country) regional and local turnout is around half of the turnout for national elections. The lower average turnout at national level in Switzerland should also be seen in the context of the regular referenda conducted on specific policy issues, for which turnout figures are also given. Citizens who feel strongly on particular issues can make their views felt on those issues; the importance of voting in

Table 3.1: Local and National Voter Turnout, in UK and Switzerland. Percentage of Population.

UK:	*National*		*Regional*		*Local*	
	1950–70	*1970–88*	*1950–70*	*1970–88*	*1950–70*	*1970–88*
	79.3	74.5	37.0	39.9	39.8	41.1

Switzerland:	*National*	*Cantonal*	*Local*
Elections:	40.1	37.5	47
Referenda (by subject):			
Culture	31.6	28.5	–
Environment	33.3	29.5	–
Taxation	37.2	32.6	38.6
Economy	40.3	37.5	47.7

Notes: 1) UK figures are for England only; in national elections the UK turnout is almost identical (79.1% and 74.6% for the two periods respectively). 2)The 1979 UK local elections were held at the same time as the national elections, and figures are therefore slightly higher. Excluding the 1979 election, average turnout was 40.6%. 3) Cantonal and local turnout figures are not available for Switzerland as a whole. They have therefore been obtained for a sample of communes in the canton of Vaud; for comparability, reported national figures refer to the same sample.

elections for representatives in the legislature is correspondingly reduced.

What do empirical studies have to say about this? There is a scholarly literature that attempts to evaluate whether particular systems of representation, or particular levels of jurisdictions take decisions that are closer to the preferences of citizens. In very broad terms, the question which is addressed is whether the observed pattern of public expenditures and decisions is more driven by the demand side (the preferences of the citizens) or the supply side (the political organizations and the bureaucracies).

Three hypotheses have been tested empirically. The first is that direct democracies will lead to decisions that are closer to the preferences of citizens than representative democracies. The intuition behind this is that citizens in direct democracies have direct and frequent control over large spending items and are more highly motivated. Second, decisions will be closer to the preferences of citizens in federal states that are tightly controlled by state and local-level bodies, at least regarding their revenues. Third, productive efficiency in the provision of public services is higher at the local level than at state or federal levels. We take these issues in turn.

3.4.1 Direct versus Representative Democracies

One way to evaluate whether actual outcomes conform well to the predictions of a decision system driven by demand is to use the theoretical insight that in simple majority voting the choice of the median voter is decisive. The importance of demand-side as opposed to supply-side considerations will be reflected in the extent to which actual outcomes in a cross-section of jurisdictions can be explained by the characteristics of the median voter.

In order to disentangle the effect of the character of the federal system from that of the direct or representative nature of the democracy, it is necessary to use a sample of jurisdictions within the same federal states. Most existing studies have focused on Switzerland and the US, where the characteristics of the representation systems vary a great deal across local jurisdictions. Results are fairly robust and suggest that the spending pattern in local jurisdictions is well explained by the characteristics of the median voter when there is a direct democracy. The association is less strong in representative democracies with optional referenda (which can be called by the citizens) and significantly poorer in representative systems (see Pommerehne, 1974; McEachern, 1978; Farnham, 1986).[5] It should be borne in mind, however, that there may be problems of sample selection (for example, size of jurisdiction may affect both its responsiveness to citizens' preferences and the feasibility of running a direct democracy); these make it wise to exercise caution before generalizing from the results.

The studies undertaken for Switzerland also found that overall spending in local jurisdictions with a representative system grew by 30% more over the 1970s than those in local jurisdictions with a direct democracy. This observation is consistent with the Leviathan version of the government failure hypothesis.

3.4.2 Federal versus Centralized States

Determining whether the budgetary decisions of federal states are more closely driven by the preferences of citizens than centralized ones involves the estimation of a demand system for various types of public outlays. The objective of this approach is to evaluate whether one can account for the observed pattern of expenditures by variables from the demand side and in particular whether the estimated demand equations meet the usual restrictions imposed on demand systems. This is obviously a very weak test, which should at best be seen as indicative.

This approach has been used for the pattern of expenditures observed in Germany and Switzerland at various levels of government over the period 1950–89. As indicated above, the main difference between the federal constitutions of Germany and Switzerland is that the latter has a much more decentralized fiscal system (so that, according to von Weizsäcker, 1987, Germany is a 'pseudo-federation'). What is found is that an almost ideal demand system (Deaton and Muellbauer, 1980) fits the Swiss data well, while respecting the usual restrictions. The fit for the German data is rather poor and a number of restrictions are violated (see Pommerehne and Kirchgässner, 1993).

Overall, this evidence lends some support to the idea that 'true' federal states (like the US and Switzerland), which involve a high degree of fiscal decentralization, may conduct public affairs more in line with citizens' preferences than others. It suggests that further fiscal consolidation in the EC may have some costs. These costs must be set against any benefits of centralization before an overall judgement on the merits of consolidation can be reached.

3.4.3 Productive Efficiency in Public Services

The evidence on the productive efficiency of public services across jurisdictions is limited to refuse collection (see Pommerehne, 1983). This evidence suggests that refuse collection by local governments is more efficient than that organized by higher levels, but also that refuse collection is organized more efficiently by local governments with a direct democracy than by those with a representative system. Since this is an instance in which it is hard to see any benefits from the coordination of policy across jurisdictions, the evidence provides a fairly conclusive argument in favour of decentralization.

3.5 The Need for Flexibility: Centralization and Policy Reform

No constitutional allocation of powers can ever foresee all the contingencies that may arise in the future. While we have discussed (in Chapter 2) reasons for thinking that the allocation of competences between the EC and its member states is more vague than it could and should be, any constitution must allow for the possibility of revision, both in the allocation of powers and in the policies those powers are used to pursue. Some policies may be flexible enough to include in their very formulation some of the changes that may need to be made: for example, it could be decided at the outset that a tax on pollution could be increased after two years if the policy had not led to rapid enough effects. But the number and complexity of possible changes is too great for them all to be explicitly foreseen.

One way to affect the way in which future changes are made is to determine a voting system. If unanimity between the parties is required for any revision, it will be relatively easy for any party that loses out from reform to block changes. (It may not be completely easy, since the exercise of a veto usually involves significant political cost.) In principle, if the status quo were inefficient, it might still be reformed if the parties benefiting from the reform were to compensate the losers, but such transfers are often difficult to make. By contrast, under qualified majority voting, reform is typically easier.

This does not imply that qualified majority voting is always preferable to unanimity. First, if a policy involves issues that one member state believes central to its interests, it may be unwilling to reach an agreement that can subsequently be revised against its will. Similarly, member states may be more willing to take difficult or costly actions to implement the policy if they can feel confident of controlling its evolution. But secondly, the power of veto can sometimes be used to accelerate reform if the continuation of a policy threatens other constraints (such as the budget constraint). As we discuss in Chapter 7 below, reform of the Common Agricultural Policy, while postponed for many years by the veto power of its net beneficiaries, was subsequently accelerated when the cost of the unreformed policy required an increase in the ceiling on member states' budgetary contributions.

A second way of influencing the character of future policy changes is to constrain them by legal doctrine, interpreted by the courts. The doctrine of subsidiarity, which expresses a presumption of jurisdiction on the side of member states, is best seen as an attempt to ensure that the future powers of the European Community institutions do not evolve in the direction of further centralization than the member states currently intend, simply because a set of Community institutions, once created, enjoys a certain bargaining power. It therefore implies a judgement that the loss of accountability this might entail would be more serious than the risk of forgoing some of the benefits of coordination because the EC remains too decentralized.[6]

Whether this judgement is reasonable is a matter on which views are likely to differ strongly, and on which empirical analysis of the past is likely by its very nature to be unable to cast much light. What we said in Chapter 2 about the way in which the Community has already acquired a federal character without the typical checks and balances characteristic of federations would tend to support the need for a burden of proof favouring member states. But our remarks about government failure should prompt caution before we assume that the terms in which the current debate are conducted necessarily reflect accurately the interests of the people of Europe as a whole. Many of the most vigorous opponents of centralization are those who currently enjoy power in nation states, and who cannot all hope to be similarly influential in European institutions in the future. Regardless of any benefits to the citizens they represent, they have an incentive to resist centralization of power. Conversely, though, many of those who enjoy power in European institutions have an interest in further centralization, which need not be in the interests of European citizens. A constitution that reflects the interests of these citizens will not necessarily be the one most favoured by any of those who, under present arrangements, claim to speak in their name.

3.6   What Kinds of Jurisdiction Should There Be?

Constitutional reform may involve changes in the allocation of power between existing jurisdictions; more fundamentally, it may even involve a change in the number and kind of jurisdictions that there are. Until now we have talked as if the size and membership of jurisdictions were predetermined. We now ask the broader questions of how the size and shape of jurisdictions should be determined, what functions jurisdictions should assume, and how many levels of jurisdiction there should be.

3.6.1 Size

Consider a jurisdiction which has a particular function – or set of functions – assigned to it. How large – in terms of population – should the jurisdiction be? The answer depends on the functions assigned to the jurisdiction, and the criteria are similar to those discussed earlier in the chapter. Heterogeneity in the preferences of the population or in access to information pull in the direction of smaller scale. Economies of scale and spillovers between regions pull in the direction of larger scale. For air traffic control, preferences are fairly homogeneous and both economies of scale and spillovers large; the converse is true for provision of parks.

3.6.2 Boundaries

Given the size of a jurisdiction, a separate issue concerns where its boundaries should lie. The principles we have previously outlined provide a guide for answering this question. Boundaries should be constructed to include within a jurisdiction a population with relatively homogeneous preferences over the function supplied. They should be consistent with efficient supply of the function, which for many functions is a matter of minimizing transport costs: garbage collectors should not have to cross a mountain range in their daily round. And they should be constructed to minimize spillovers between different jurisdictions. For example, we discuss in Chapter 4 the way in which the magnitude of the problem posed by fiscal competition depends on the mobility of capital and labour. Thus a criterion for construction of boundaries is the cross-boundary mobility of labour.

Existing regional and national boundaries – themselves determined in part by geography – often meet these criteria, but there are clearly circumstances in which they do not. For example, cultural provision for the Celts might be best supplied by a jurisdiction spanning parts of Ireland, Britain and France. Homogeneity of preferences amongst this population and increasing returns in service provision may outweigh costs imposed by geographical dispersion of the jurisdiction. Notice also that in this example illustrates how levels of jurisdiction need not follow a hierarchical tree structure. A Celtic cultural jurisdiction could operate under several national governments (though it could not do so and simultaneously enjoy an unfettered power to tax).

The consequences of economic integration itself may also suggest the need to redraw jurisdictional boundaries. It is sometimes suggested that integration may lead to a redrawing of the economic geography of Europe, with the growth of cross-national zones of economic activity. Within such zones there may well be reduced transport costs, increased factor mobility, and perhaps increasing homogenization of preferences, all suggesting that – for some functions – the zone forms a natural jurisdictional unit. Again, such jurisdictions may cut across several national governments.

3.6.3 Membership Criteria

So far we have implicitly defined jurisdictions in geographical terms, but geographical location is not the only possible criterion for membership of a jurisdiction. A Welsh jurisdiction could cover the population of Wales or the Welsh-speaking population. Evidently the criterion used for membership of the jurisdiction depends on the function of the jurisdiction. For many functions efficient supply dictates that the membership criterion is geographical; for example, provision of local public goods or defence. But for other functions homogeneity of preferences may assume greater relative importance, and geography is then a poor membership criterion.

It hardly needs stressing that changes in the kind and number of jurisdictions in any constitutional arrangement are some of the most difficult and violently disputed decisions that any society has to take. Space forbids here a more detailed consideration of this aspect of constitutional reform, but Drèze (1993) discusses proposals designed to make secessions less painful by restricting them to efficiency-enhancing changes rather than purely redistributive ones.

3.7 Centralization, Decentralization and the Second-best

Our discussion in this chapter has emphasized a fundamental trade-off. Centralization enables the benefits of policy coordination to be realized when it is not credible that simple cooperative agreement will achieve these; it also incurs the costs of loss of accountability to the needs and interests of differing localities. It can hardly be stressed too strongly, however, that the conclusions must be tempered by an awareness that all actual constitutional arrangements are second-best systems, where multiple inefficiencies interact. Some apparently desirable changes can sometimes make matters worse if they interact with pre-existing distortions of a different kind. Two examples can illustrate the need for caution. The first concerns the danger that cooperation on some aspects of a policy may worsen the efficiency costs associated with non-cooperation in other areas (see Gatsios and Seabright, 1989). For example, coordinated reductions in trade barriers may provoke a 'subsidy war' that leads to the most heavily subsidized and inefficient producers driving out the more efficient (Winters, 1988). There is evidence that the policing of fraud against the Common Agricultural Policy has been very weak because each member state is required to undertake its own policing but must hand over the amounts recovered to the Community budget (House of Lords, 1989). Similar risks may apply to the incentives to prevent tax evasion, where the authorities charged with doing so see a significant proportion of tax revenue transferred between their jurisdiction and others.

The other instance of the second-best problem we shall cite is central to the nature of fiscal competition. Raising taxes from factors of production to finance public goods requires in a second-best world that some factors of production yield more tax revenue than is needed to finance the marginal public goods and services they consume. Even when direct spillovers between countries in a certain area are negligible (say in some aspects of environmental protection), the fact that policy changes can influence factor mobility between jurisdictions means there are indirect spillovers whereby the decisions of one authority affect the size of another authority's tax base. This particular second-best problem is so important that we shall discuss it in Chapter 4. In the remaining chapters, however, we shall allude to problems of the second-best where appropriate, but we will argue in general that the principles outlined in this chapter provide a reasonably practical guide to the benefits and costs of centralized and decentralized government.

3.8 Conclusion

While pointing to the existence of a fundamental trade-off between the coordination benefits of centralization and the accountability benefits of decentralization, this chapter has emphasized that there are many complex factors at work, and the balance of advantages is likely to vary greatly from case to case. There are no simple punchlines about centralization, and therefore none about subsidiarity. Power in a modern state is and should be distributed across several layers of government according to the comparative advantage of each in respect of the different functions the modern state performs. Later chapters in this Report will illustrate this claim in detail for some of the most important of these many functions.

We have drawn attention to the claim of Tiebout and others that mobility of citizens between jurisdictions can have important benefits in sorting populations according to their preferences for public goods, and in rendering government more accountable. But the state envisaged by Tiebout is something of a parody of the state as we know it in the real world. It is more like a firm, catering to the tastes of a homogeneous local population for a differentiated product that can most easily be interpreted as a bundle of public goods and which is supplied to them at marginal cost. It does no more than offer citizens at home what a competitive travel agency offers them when they take a vacation.

Modern states in reality have diverse populations and produce many public goods under increasing returns to scale. These two factors mean that, to finance their legitimate activities (including both the supply of such public goods and the transfer of resources between citizens in different circumstances), governments must raise from significant groups in the population amounts of tax revenue well in excess of the marginal cost of supplying them with goods and services. To the extent that these groups are mobile between states, competition to attract them (and the surplus they bring with them) may drive tax rates below the levels required to enable the state to conduct its legitimate business. This is exactly like the observation that competition between more than one firm in an industry that is naturally monopolistic may threaten the ability of all firms to cover their costs, and hence to survive at all.

While limitations on the mobility of taxable factors of production are part of the reason why populations are diverse in the first place, increases in this mobility may exacerbate rather than alleviate the fiscal problems faced by modern states. Centralization of the power to tax may offset such increases in mobility to the extent that factors remain less mobile between the central jurisdiction and outside than they are between its subsidiary jurisdictions. In Chapter 4 we tackle the question whether increased factor mobility in an integrated European economy is likely to threaten the ability of the state to command the resources it needs to carry out its appropriate functions, and if so whether centralization of fiscal sovereignty can be expected to offer any comfort.

Notes

[1] We are not concerned here with arguments that base decentralization on the rights of localities.

[2] There may, of course, be good reasons for the inflexibility of centralized policies, in that inflexibility may be part of the response to, rather than the essence of, the failure of accountability at the centre. For instance, if income taxes could be explicitly differentiated according to locality, this might set off flurries of lobbying on the part of those localities with less favourable treatment. Nevertheless, US Congressional budget negotiations typically involve inducements to wavering Senators and Representatives not in the form of direct transfers to their districts, but of indirect (and inefficient) subsidies and inducements to activities that happen to be locally concentrated. This shows that avoiding the explicit differentiation of policy by locality is hardly a miracle cure for rent-seeking. More significantly, in many political cultures explicit differentiation by locality is seen as very divisive (much as explicit differentiation by race or gender may be). The resulting inflexibility can, however, have significant efficiency costs.

[3] There are interesting parallels here (some of which motivate the model in Appendix 3.2) with the divorce between ownership and control in modern corporations and the consequent devices (ranging from shareholder actions to takeover bids) to mitigate the costs of managerial discretion. Voting for local governments is similar to voting for boards of directors; mobility between jurisdictions is analogous to the decision of dissatisfied shareholders to sell their shares (which may in turn be what provokes a takeover bid).

[4] Some people would argue that something like this has happened within the European Community over environmental policy: environmental interests that had little weight at national level have been more successful in influencing the European Commission – perhaps because the Commission, being less politically secure, has been more aware of the need to respond to the changing public perception of environmental issues.

[5] Santerre (1986) looking at US counties even shows that counties with a representative democracy have lower land values, to such an extent that marginal consumer-voter is compensated for the relative inefficiency of his/her government.

[6] It may also be interpreted as a reaction to a perceived tendency to justify centralization whenever there are significant coordination benefits, without giving proper attention to its accountability costs. If it is intended merely as a reminder to take accountability problems seriously, the principle of subsidiarity is hard to fault.

Appendix 3.1

The Invisible Foot: Does the Tiebout Hypothesis Justify Decentralized Government?

A3.1.1 The Case Against Central Government

Suppose public goods are supplied by a single central government. Its politicians and bureaucrats pursue their own interests, which do not coincide exactly with the wider public interest. In such circumstances, the provision of public goods and the taxes to finance them are unlikely to be efficient. Individual citizens can express dissatisfaction by lobbying the central government or by voting in national elections. Neither mechanism is likely to lead to an efficient outcome. Individuals lobby only if the expected benefits of so doing exceed the costs. Lobbyists represent small groups whose interests are concentrated – not large groups across which the effects are widely dispersed, making free-riding irresistible. For example, domestic producer groups lobby governments for protection against cheap imports; domestic consumer groups are unable to organize lobbying against such protection. When individuals vote at elections, they typically face a choice of two or three packages of public goods. They cannot express their preferences about the levels of provision of specific public goods. Since a particular individual's vote has an insignificant effect on the outcome of an election, it is in any case highly unlikely that individuals will base their voting decisions on good information about the costs and benefits of public goods.

Even a government whose interests did coincide perfectly with the wider public interest would have problems choosing what level of public goods to provide. Asking individuals to report the strength of their preference for public goods will not necessarily elicit truthful answers. If individuals' tax liability is unrelated to the degree of preference they report, they will tend to exaggerate the benefit they derive from public goods. If it is related to the degree of preference they report, most individuals will understate the benefit they derive, since they can thereby reduce their tax burden while having only a negligible impact on the overall level of the good provided.

A3.1.2 The Tiebout Hypothesis

If the single central government were replaced by a number of autonomous decentralized governments in different regions, individuals could then express dissatisfaction with the allocation of resources to public goods by voting with their feet: they could move to another jurisdiction offering a preferred bundle of public goods and tax liabilities. The Tiebout hypothesis is the claim that an equilibrium outcome of a situation in which individuals move costlessly in search of their most preferred bundle of public goods between different decentralized governments, each of which provides a particular mix of public goods financed by a uniform lump-sum tax on the residents within its jurisdiction, will be Pareto-efficient. This hypothesis provides some of the theoretical muscle for the view that decentralized government is superior to central government. It might be regarded as providing a particularly simple interpretation of the subsidiarity principle: all government decisions should be decentralized in order to achieve an efficient outcome. Unfortunately, the conditions under which the Tiebout hypothesis is correct are so restrictive as to make it unhelpful for the analysis of actual governments (Bewley, 1981).

To explain why, we begin by examining the Tiebout hypothesis in more detail. If a particular bundle of public goods must be consumed in a particular place, it may be possible to prevent individuals from other jurisdictions from consuming public goods provided in a particular jurisdiction. The tax a resident has to pay to the government of a region can then serve as a price paid for the bundle of public goods provided in that region. In principle, therefore, if mobility between regions is costless, individuals can be faced with a set of different bundles of public goods and associated prices (reflecting the cost and extent of provision) by means of a number of different regional governments. With a sufficient number of regional governments, each individual can choose a preferred bundle by choosing where to reside. By sorting themselves into homogeneous groups, each consuming their preferred bundles of goods, individuals satisfy their preferences subject to their budget constraints. It is not possible to increase efficiency through alternative allocations of public and private good consumption. A large enough number of different regional governments also ensures that competition between them prevents regional politicians and bureaucrats pursuing their own interests at the expense of citizens, so no resources are wasted by internal inefficiencies in governments.

A3.1.3 Limitations of the Tiebout Hypothesis

As a proof of the efficiency of the invisible foot, the hypothesis requires a great many assumptions, as the above account made clear. First, individuals must be costlessly mobile between regions. Second, there must be no spillovers between localities (e.g. use of public parks by tourists from other localities). Third, there must be an adequate selection of localities to offer all the conceivable bundles of public goods: even with only four public goods, each supplied in four possible amounts, that would imply a need for 4^4 or 256 localities to cater for all possible tastes. Fourth, and related, such a large number of localities could produce public goods efficiently only if there were no scale economies in the production of such goods. These four objections already undermine much of the power of the Tiebout rationale for decentralization.

But yet more assumptions are needed to sustain the hypothesis. How, in this argument, do regional governments decide which bundle of public goods to provide? The Tiebout model implicitly assumes that they maximize profits – but what does this mean in the context of local government? Having begun from concerns about the vulnerability of central government to special interests, such concerns are entirely neglected in the account of regional government.

A final, yet critical, consideration is the role of geography. The function of a region in the Tiebout model is to exclude non-residents from consuming public goods for which they do not pay. Yet in practice this exclusion mechanism is far from perfect, thereby divorcing in part the essential connection between public goods consumed and taxes paid.

Moreover, in the production of other goods, there are often advantages in the clustering together of individuals who share production skills. If these workers have very different tastes for public goods they may be driven to reside so far apart that sharing a work location becomes impossible: the Tiebout hypothesis implicitly requires that productivity is independent of location effects. A similar argument applies to locational consumption: people who like mountains and art will remain unsatisfied if all public art galleries are on plains.

We therefore conclude that the Tiebout hypothesis points us towards useful insights and alerts us to some considerations that our analysis might otherwise have omitted. In particular, it highlights two great virtues of decentralized government. First, by differentiating public good consumption according to location it improves the incentives for individuals to reveal their true preferences for public goods. Second, it strengthens the accountability of local government by adding to the electoral power of citizens an additional mechanism: a show of feet. If governments always pursued the public interest anyway, only the first virtue would matter. And ironically, if the exact assumptions of the hypothesis were correct, the second virtue would be unimportant, since if there are constant returns to scale it does not matter to a local government if some of its citizens leave. In the world as we know it, both virtues of decentralization matter. But a model as artificial as the Tiebout model does not help us to judge how much they matter, still less to weigh them against the costs of decentralization (such as spillovers and loss of scale economies) which it assumes entirely away.

Appendix 3.2

Centralization and Accountability

The literature on corporate finance has recently explored ways in which the allocation of rights of control over a firm's assets in various circumstances to different interested parties (such as to shareholders and to creditors) can be understood as a means of providing the right incentives to managers to exert their efforts towards an efficient management of the firm's assets rather than the pursuit of their own concerns (see Aghion and Bolton, 1992; Dewatripont and Tirole, 1993). The idea is that when contracts are incomplete it is not possible to specify in advance who should take what actions under all circumstances; the best one can do may be to specify who should be responsible, on the basis that the specified party is the one most likely to have the right interests at heart. The choice between centralized and decentralized forms of government can be treated in a similar vein.

Consider a simple model (drawn from Seabright, 1993) in which the population in a certain country is divided between two regions, whose people will elect a government. This may be either a government for each region or a single central government. The people and the governments are risk neutral. After election the governments have to implement policies which we can represent by two numbers; these are either chosen separately and simultaneously by the separate governments, or jointly by the central government. The population of each region would prefer higher values of both numbers (including that chosen by the government of the other region), but the governments would prefer lower values which involve less effort. The actions of the governments are not directly observable by the population, however. These governments must therefore be induced to undertake such effort by the threat that they will not be re-elected if the populations are not satisfied with their levels of welfare. Re-election has a certain value for them (the spoils of office), but the population's welfare is also affected by additive but unobserved region-specific shocks. If their welfare net of these shocks falls short of some reservation level C (which can be interpreted as the welfare they might expect from a rival political party) they will wish to throw out the government. Regional governments will fail to be re-elected if the welfare level of the population in the region falls below C; a central government, however, will fail to be re-elected only if both regions' welfare falls below C.

Centralization in this model therefore involves two features. Its advantage is that by allowing the central government to control both policy variables it internalizes any spillovers between the regions. Its disadvantage is that any one region loses its ability to eject the government purely according to its own preferences. We can compare the incentives faced by governments to act in the interests of their electors under the two regimes:

Under Regional Government:

Marginal disutility of effort		Value of re-election	×	Marginal increase in probability that region is satisfied
	=			

Under Central Government:

Marginal disutility of effort		Value of re-election	×	Marginal increase in probability that region is satisfied	Probability that × this region's welfare determines re-election
	=				

Plus Value of re-election × Spillover on welfare of other region × Effect of welfare increase on probability that other region is satisfied × Probability that other region's welfare determines re-election

What kinds of conclusion can be drawn from this analysis? Some are obvious, some less so:

First, it confirms the basic intuition that the case for centralization is strengthened if there are significant spillovers between regions.

Second, it also gives a precise sense to the notion that the cost of centralization is a loss of local accountability. This is interpreted as the fact that the welfare of a region now has a probability of less than one of being the decisive factor in whether or not the government is re-elected.

Third, a less obvious conclusion is that a positive correlation between region-specific shocks strengthens the case for centralization. To see this, note that the probability that any region's welfare is decisive in whether or not the central government is re-elected is the probability that the other region is dissatisfied, conditional on this region's being dissatisfied. And this conditional probability increases with the correlation of the shocks to the two regions.

Fourth, this is not at all the same as saying that regional similarity strengthens the case for centralization. If differences between regions are incorporated in their different utility functions or the different distributions of their region-specific shocks (variables that are known to populations and governments before any decisions are taken), then both regional and central governments are entirely capable of setting different values of the policy variables to reflect these differences. Centralization makes the regional differentiation of policy neither easier nor more difficult. It is the degree of correlation of shocks (which are not observed by the populations) that affects the degree of centralization. To put it another way, what weakens local accountability is not the risk that regions will require different policies, but the risk that regions will be differentially satisfied with whatever policies they have.

Fifth, the more 'entrenched' governments are, in that the voters are less likely to wish to eject them, the stronger is the case for regional as opposed to central government. This is because if one region is unlikely to want to eject its government it is relatively even more unlikely that both regions will wish to do so, so the loss of accountability from centralization is relatively greater.

Sixth, the interest of citizens in one or other form of government is not necessarily shared by their political representatives. Local politicians will lose, and central politicians gain, from centralization, whatever the benefits to their citizens.

Finally, a choice between centralized and decentralized forms of government need not always be made once and for all, but can sometimes be undertaken on a case-be-case basis if it is possible to estimate some of the relevant variables (such as the size of the spillovers). Merger control, which we discuss in Chapter 7, is a good example where powers are allocated according to the estimated importance of spillovers in each case.

4 Factor Mobility, Fiscal Competition and the Survival of the Nation State

The nation state might not survive ever-closer market integration within the EC. How could the fiscal sovereignty of individual member states ebb away? Enhanced mobility of capital and labour leads to fiscal competition among member states. Mobile factors flee taxation and look for host countries offering high levels of infrastructure and public goods. States can no longer turn a fiscal profit on mobile factors. Government is reduced in scale and in its power to redistribute. Scale is reduced because raising taxes is hard and because fiscal competition bids down the provision of public services. Redistribution is reduced because some mobile factors, including human and physical capital, no longer pay high taxes, and because a reduced provision of public goods, which are necessarily consumed equally by everyone, hits the poor proportionately harder than the rich.

If factor mobility is high, locating fiscal powers in the nation state will imply the erosion of the welfare state (not just redistributive taxation but also provision of public services, social protection and insurance, including commitment to macroeconomic stabilization policy). Nation states will lose much of their efficacy and be driven back towards pure Tiebout states offering the bundles of public provision that mobile factors are prepared to purchase.

Could centralization help? If factors are mobile within the EC but not across its external borders, fiscal competition would not operate at the EC level as a whole. The choice may be between a decentralized Community with a welfare state substantially less extensive than at present or a centralized Community that retains the option of preserving the welfare state at present levels. Inevitably, attitudes towards the appropriate degree of centralization of the Community would then be bound up with attitudes towards the welfare state itself. Given the diagnosis, the two are inseparable.

Redistribution is not the only issue. Inefficiency means that in principle everyone could benefit if we did things differently. Factor mobility and fiscal competition create the potential for inefficiency. Each member state, by neglecting the effects of its actions on other member states, may drive tax rates and public provision below the levels that best reflect the wishes of EC citizens as a whole.

Factor mobility affects not just equity and efficiency but also accountability. The principle of subsidiarity reflects a presumption of significant problems in accountability. Factor mobility affects the ease with which citizens can sort themselves into homogeneous groups, a recipe for greater accountability at local level, but it implies that those who obtain fiscal benefits today may less reliably be there to pay for them tomorrow, which is potentially a recipe for weaker accountability.

To investigate how factor mobility affect fiscal policy, and hence at which level of government it makes sense to locate fiscal control, Section 4.1 discusses the degree of factor mobility that the EC faces today and might face in the future. Section 4.2 introduces some key principles of tax design as a guide to the incentives that will govern fiscal policy in such circumstances, and it explains how factor mobility is likely to affect fiscal structure. Section 4.3 analyses fiscal competition among member states and the consequences for efficiency and equity, developing the case for centralization of fiscal policy. Section 4.4 reconsiders the costs of centralization and how the tension between centralization and decentralization should be reflected in fiscal design. Subsequent sections discuss applications of this analysis to areas of fiscal policy.

4.1 Factor Mobility

Achieving the 'four freedoms' – the mobility of goods, services, labour and capital – was an objective of the Treaty of Rome. With the completion of the single market, the EC has substantially realized this objective. Barriers to the movement of goods and factors have been dramatically reduced, with consequent increases in mobility. But to what extent? Freedom to move does not guarantee that a good or factor will move.

Within the EC, product mobility has been substantially boosted by the completion of the single market on 1 January 1993: this not only permits the unfettered movement of goods within the EC but even creates possibilities for cross-border shopping. The mobility of factors of production may be less obvious. Although many factors seem rather immobile, including land and large parts of the labour force, closer inspection tends to raise estimates of the extent of their mobility. Financial and real capital are highly mobile. When Germany tried to introduce a moderate 10% source tax on capital in 1989, at least DM 100 billion of financial capital fled within a year-and-a-half (Nöhrbass and Raab, 1990).

Is capital mobile globally or just within the EC? The global mobility of real capital is significant, but its mobility within the EC is clearly much higher. The single market guarantees EC market access to EC producers, which is never guaranteed for those who invest in production facilities elsewhere but hope to sell into the EC: residual uncertainties about future tariff and regulatory treatment never disappear (CEPR, 1992). Thus, it is easier for EC capital to migrate elsewhere within the EC than to move outside.

It is usually assumed that labour mobility within the EC is low. Flows of labour between countries are small relative to the stock of workers in each country. Language, culture and the costs of physical displacement do indeed segment labour markets. Table 4.1 seems to suggest that labour mobility in Europe today is a phenomenon largely restricted to within national boundaries.

At the beginning of 1991, EC citizens residing in other EC countries made up about 2.3% of the total Community population. This proportion

Table 4.1: Residence and Migration Within the EC. 1990–91.
Thousands of People.

	Residents in 1991			*1990–91 Increases in Residents from Other EC*
	Nationals	*Other EC*	*Non-EC*	
Belgium	9,082	551	353	9
Denmark	4,985	28	133	0
Germany	74,235	1,439	3,903	114
Greece	9,090	54	175	3
Spain	38,510	273	–	32
France	53,055	1,312	2,285	3
Ireland	3,436	69	19	4
Italy	56,975	149	632	45
Luxembourg	269	103	13	−3
Netherlands	14,318	168	524	0
Portugal	9,750	29	79	2
UK	54,276	782	1,024	−124

Source: *Eurostat*, 1993.

had been higher in the 1970s (7% in 1970), mostly due to emigration from Italy, Spain and Portugal.

But it has been steadily on the decrease since then, with recent inflows into Italy and Spain (Simon, 1991). Table 4.1 shows, for each of the twelve member states for 1991, the inflows and outflows of residents from or into the EC(12). Absolute flows of EC citizens are *tiny* except for Germany (inflow) and the UK (outflow). In percentage terms, inflows or outflows do not exceed 0.25% except for Luxembourg. Even more telling, 1.2 million Italians moved yearly from one Italian city or region to another during the 1980s while the annual emigration of Italians was only 50,000 per year (EC, 1992).

This apparent labour market segmentation should not be exaggerated, however. First, the data were collected before the liberalization of intra-EC migration. Second, data such as those shown in Table 4.1 apply to *net* flows and are compatible with substantial *gross* flows in both directions. Third, even if such flows are low, competitive pressure and the degree of substitutability concern marginal not average responses to change: to demonstrate that averages are low does not in itself prove that marginal effects are negligible. Fourth, cross-border transmission may be vigorous even though little mobility is observed *ex post*. Policies may change precisely to *deter* mobility, as for example with German unification. Finally, labour may have some of the putty-clay properties normally attributed to capital. Those set in their ways, with cultural and personal roots, may indeed be pretty immobile, but newcomers have fewer locational constraints. A Europe admitting immigrants in the 1990s, whether by design or because policing external borders is difficult, may be a Europe in which labour mobility is somewhat higher than normal.

Having discussed the limitations to direct evidence on factor movements, we now turn to evidence that is indirect but more reliable as a guide to mobility. When two commodities are perfect substitututes, arbitrage ensures that they have the same price. Focusing on prices rather than quantities is more informative. Thus, we may learn more about the degree of international substitutablity from looking at tax rates or factor incomes than by looking at international flows of factors.

Figure 4.1 shows the tax rates on corporate profits within the G7 countries. It certainly points to a reduction in both the mean level and the dispersion of tax rates on this form of capital income, and it is therefore consistent with the view that capital mobility has already increased substantially. Of course, Figure 4.1 may also reflect a swing in political mood towards less intervention and greater reliance on market forces in general; but it is part of the hypothesis examined in this chapter that changes in factor mobility may be one of the causes of changes in the trade-offs that politicians face. Figure 4.1 also reminds us that, although capital mobility has increased substantially within the EC, it has probably increased at the global level as well.

Figure 4.1: Basic Corporate Tax Rates in the G7 Countries. 1972–92.

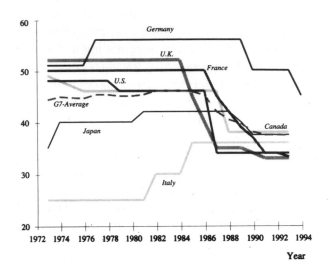

Sources: Coopers & Lybrand, *International Tax Summaries*, various issues; International Bureau of Fiscal Documentation, *Tax News Service,* various issues; Peat, Marwick, Mitchell & Co: *European Taxation,* 1979; Deloitte, Haskins & Sells (UK): *Taxation in Europe,* various issues.
Note: Germany has decided to reduce its rate to 45% by 1 January 1994.

What about labour mobility? How large might it become, and how much is this likely to constrain redistributive policy? Some ideas about the future of labour mobility in Europe can be gleaned by examining what goes on today in Switzerland. The country is small, so internal geographical barriers to mobility are low. There are also three distinct regions, each with its own language, and Swiss children become fluent in more than one language. If education can easily overcome language and cultural barriers, we should anticipate high labour mobility among Swiss cantons, little income inequality across cantons, and little opportunity for redistribution within cantons. This might be a model of what a truly integrated Europe would look like.

Figure 4.2: Income per Capita in Swiss Cantons and EC Countries. 1988.

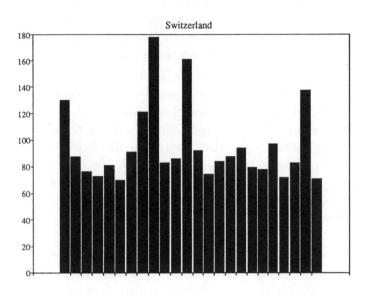

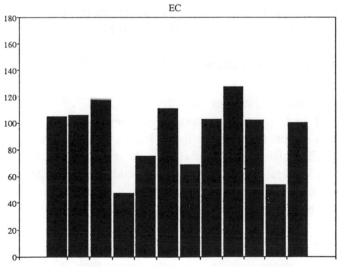

Sources: Dafflon (1990) and *European Economy.*

What are the facts? Figure 4.2 shows the dispersion of per capita income levels in the different Swiss cantons (setting the mean at 100), and for comparison shows per capita income levels in each EC country (also scaled to have a mean of 100). These are roughly equally dispersed; a formal statistical analysis reveals that the standard deviation across Swiss cantons is actually slightly higher than across EC countries.

Obviously we have to be careful in comparing cantons with countries. Essentially, the EC data remind us that countries like Germany, Denmark and France have average per capita incomes that are about four times that of Portugal. The Swiss data imply that the dispersion of income levels across cantons is roughly comparable. *Prima facie*, this seems to suggest that labour mobility is rather *low*. If the Swiss don't move canton – for reasons of language, culture, habit or whatever – do we expect substantial movement among countries of the EC?

Indeed, we could pursue this train of thought a little further. If labour mobility is high among Swiss cantons, opportunities for redistribution within them should be low, and redistributive spending by cantons correspondingly low. In contrast, if labour mobility is low, cantons should be able to engage in redistribution within their own jurisdictions should they so wish, without provoking a complete emigration of their tax bases or an inflow of migrants anticipating welfare benefits.

Table 4.2 shows data on transfer payments by government in Switzerland and, for comparison, West Germany, for three tiers of government from federal down to local. Several features deserve comment. First, we expect mobility to be greatest at local level and smallest at federal level. Transfers should therefore be easiest to undertake at federal level and hardest at local level. This is borne out by the data for both countries.

Second, although transfers in Switzerland were relatively low in 1960, there has been strong growth in transfers since then at both federal *and* canton levels, and by 1989 the Swiss cantons undertook more transfers than their counterparts, the much larger German Länder. Although not

Table 4.2: Government Transfer Payments.
1960–89. Percentage of GDP.

		1960	1970	1980	1989
Switzerland:	Federal	1.3	1.7	3.3	3.1
	Canton	1.1	1.7	2.3	3.6
	Local	0.6	0.7	0.9	1.0
	Total	3.0	4.1	6.5	7.7
West Germany:	Federal	4.2	5.1	6.4	5.9
	Land	2.3	2.6	3.3	2.9
	Local	0.8	1.0	1.2	1.2
	Total	7.3	8.7	10.9	10.0

Source: Pommerehne and Kirchgässner (1993).

conclusive, this tends to corroborate the message of Figure 4.2. Inter-canton migration is not very large; hence cantons have scope to redistribute income internally. Putting it differently, the Swiss case tends to support those who think that language, culture and history will continue to provide significant barriers to labour migration by EC citizens within the EC.

Such considerations may not apply to recent immigrants to the EC. In particular, the fall of the Iron Curtain faces Western Europe with the possibility of large-scale immigration whose limits are not yet visible. Those who have left their home countries and have been legally accepted into the EC are in principle perfectly mobile among countries, and they can be expected to seek out places that would maximize their living standards. Illegal immigrants are a different matter since they are neither perfectly mobile among EC countries nor eligible for social benefits in the country in which they happen to reside. The extent to which mobility of recent immigrants will add to the fiscal pressures upon the EC's nation states will therefore depend critically on how much legal immigration the EC is willing to accept. Its willingness to do so may well be influenced by humanitarian considerations, especially if civil conflict spreads widely in the East. On the other hand, concern for the fiscal consequences may provoke political pressures for a restrictive policy towards legal immigration from regions that, though poor, are not engaged in civil war.

Given its potential importance, it is perhaps surprising that research on factor mobility is still in its infancy. There are econometric studies highlighting the effects on migration of wage differentials, relative unemployment rates and so on. But migration decisions, for both labour and capital, entail consideration of a range of costs and benefits, including for example public goods and environmental capital provided as well as taxes incurred; and because there are fixed costs in moving, such decisions must typically consider the anticipated stream of costs and benefits over rather a long horizon.

For these reasons, we can as yet cite no econometric estimates that would encapsulate in a few parameters the judgements we seek to make about the readiness or otherwise of factors to move. We have to rely on the more impressionistic evidence discussed above. Our ensuing analysis assumes high mobility of physical capital within the EC and low labour mobility between the EC and the rest of world. (We see little prospect of substantial emigration of EC citizens; but it is harder to be certain about the success of EC policy in restricting immigration.) The evidence to date is insufficient to quantify the extents to which capital is less mobile across the EC's external borders than within the EC, or labour more mobile within the EC than across its external borders. Continuing trends of cheaper transport and communication in themselves will be forces for greater mobility in the long run, and the potential for legal immigration from the East may considerably increase even the mobility of labour among EC countries. Having indicated our judgements about the factor mobility relevant to the Community, we shall try to indicate as we go along where different judgements might alter our conclusions.

4.2   Principles of Tax Design

Taxes drive a wedge between the price the consumer-buyer pays and the price the producer-seller receives. Since the efficiency of markets rests on their ability to bring marginal production costs and marginal consumer benefits into line simply by getting producers and consumers to face the same prices, taxes generally create distortions that give rise to inefficiency. For example, consumers buy cars up to the point that the marginal benefit of another car equals its price, but this is a higher price than the net-of-tax price relevant to car manufacturers in deciding production levels and thereby the marginal production cost of cars. With the marginal benefit of a car exceeding its marginal cost, we could make a social profit by producing more cars, a free lunch that allows everyone to be better off.

Although taxes create distortions, we cannot do without taxes. Governments need to supply public goods (defence, infrastructure, welfare services) and we may also want them to redistribute. Given our desire for such things, we cannot live in a first-best, distortion-free world. We live in a world of many distortions. Taxes introduce distortionary wedges; provision of public goods or financial transfers may also affect incentives adversely. In this difficult world of the second-best, we can still say rather a lot about the efficient design of fiscal policy. Because a distortion-induced departure in the quantity of a product from its ideal 'first-best' level generally does more damage the larger the departure from that level, it is efficient to spread distortions around: lots of little mistakes in quantities hurt less than a few big ones.

This insight has a direct implication for tax rates. When demand and supply of a particular product are both elastic, a given tax wedge will have a big effect on the quantity produced and purchased, a large distortion; inelastic supply or demand implies that a tax wedge of the same size has much less impact on the amount produced and sold. Thus, to raise a given amount of tax revenue while minimizing the distortions caused by tax wedges, tax rates should be highest where quantities are least sensitive to prices and tax rates, and they should be lowest where

Figure 4.3: The Inefficiency of Taxing Mobile Factors.

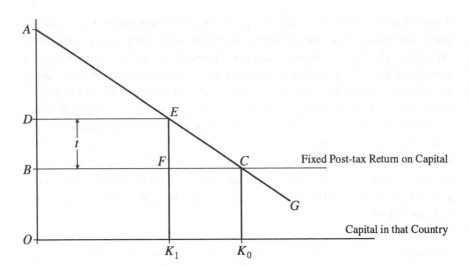

quantities are most sensitive to prices and tax rates. This general principle finds practical expression in most countries' tax structures. For example, demand for alcohol and tobacco is relatively insensitive to price; it is therefore efficient for tax rates on these products to be very high.

At the opposite extreme, things that are infinitely responsive should be completely untaxed. Figure 4.3 makes this point in a particularly vivid way. Imagine capital is perfectly mobile but labour is not. The horizontal axis shows the quantity of capital in a particular EC country, the vertical axis shows the return on this capital. AG shows that the return on capital falls as more capital is employed with the fixed amount of labour. Given perfect capital mobility, capital has to earn the going post-tax rate of return, OB; otherwise, it all departs.

In the absence of capital taxation, capital employed is K_0, earning $OBCK_0$ in total. Since the country's total income is the area $OACK_0$, the immobile factors earn ABC. Now suppose immobile voter-workers urge their government to impose a tax on capital. Some capital leaves the country in order that the lower remaining capital K_1 can now earn a pre-tax return OD to ensure that capital still achieves its required post-tax return OB. Capital income net of tax is $OBFK_1$. $BDEF$ is tax revenue available for redistribution to immobile factors, and ADE is the income of immobile factors when they can work with a capital stock K_1. So in total immobile factors get $ABFE$; when the rate is t, but this is less than the ABC they received when completely mobile capital was completely untaxed.

This example makes two general points. First, it emphasizes a key point in the economics of taxation: the burden or incidence of a tax does not necessarily fall on the good, service or factor from which the tax is collected. Here, mobile factors are taxed, but immobile factors bear all the consequences of the distortion. (The avoidable waste, the triangle EFC, is subtracted from their incomes.) Second, it confirms that it is inefficient to tax mobile factors heavily.

Suppose a nation state is raising tax revenue in the manner it believes to be most efficient given its objectives. What happens if barriers to the movement of products and factors are now reduced within the EC? In general, considerations such as that underlying Figure 4.3 become more relevant. Tax rates on mobile factors and products are reduced, and revenues from these sources fall. The second-best now requires the state to find the least-bad compromise in its other activities. In part this will mean cutting back on public goods and transfer payments, in part it will mean raising taxes further on immobile factors to avoid concentrating the whole burden of adjustment on cuts in government spending. While this appears to each individual government the best response it can make, however, we show in Section 4.3 that it may be possible to do better collectively.

We conclude our discussion of the second-best by emphasizing the pervasiveness of its implications. Efficiency is relentless in its search to spread appropriately the consequences of unavoidable distortions. For example, mobile capital may care about not only the tax rate to which it will be subject but also the regulatory structure that will govern production with that capital. A country may have to offer mobile capital 'the going rate' in international terms, but this package may allow variations. In industries that pollute the environment, this 'going rate' may be compatible with higher taxes if accompanied by suitably looser environmental regulation, or vice versa. Second-best calculations will evaluate the damage each of these components does elsewhere in the economy and may prefer packages whose composition is the least distortionary.

Taxation usually treats equals equally. Making concessions to mobile factors is therefore most damaging when there are lots of immobile factors to which the same concessions will have to apply. For example, if old capital cannot be unscrewed, it is unfortunate that capital tax rates are driven down by the market forces that affect investment; if the old and new capital could have been treated separately, it would still have been possible to tax old capital.

In such circumstances, it seems plausible that countries may be able to discriminate more easily with regulatory policy or public goods than with tax policy. Regulatory standards or public good provision can be targeted on the particular needs of the marginal inflowing factor without creating large distortions elsewhere in the economy. If so, second-best considerations suggest that each individual country will think it efficient to use combinations of policy in this manner.

4.3 Fiscal Externalities

4.3.1 Inefficiency from Externalities

Fiscal externalities arise when the fiscal actions of one state affect the interests of other states. Since each ignores the external effect of its actions, the outcome is likely to be inefficient from the collective viewpoint. Cooperation among EC countries, through coordination or centralization, can in principle benefit them all.

There are two channels through which fiscal externalities can operate. First, one member state's fiscal policy (interpreted widely to include ancillary regulatory policy of the kind just discussed), by attracting mobile factors, diminishes the tax bases of other member states without taking this into account. In a second-best world, a lower tax base means there is a need to compensate by introducing new distortions: less mobile factors face higher taxation, and public good provision becomes inefficiently low. These are the distortions induced by, but ignored by, the policies of other member states.

This externality, through its effects on other countries' tax bases, normally leads to inefficiently low tax rates on factors that are mobile only within the EC. In relatively inelastic supply to the EC as a whole, they should bear a relatively high tax throughout the EC. In general, the inefficiency of uncoordinated policy is more severe the greater the disparity between the responsiveness of the tax base to national and EC-wide taxes.

The second type of fiscal externality involves effects of a member state's tax policy on the prices faced and incomes earned by citizens of other member states. For example, an origin-based commodity tax imposed by a member state on a good which it exports to others may raise the price faced by consumers in these importing countries. Individual member states are small relative to the EC, however, let alone in relation to world markets. In practice, such externalities are therefore likely to have only minor effects on the fiscal decisions of member states.

Inefficiency from these externalities may extend well beyond the level of taxation. The structure of taxation may also be distorted: inefficiently low taxation of mobile tax bases will be compensated by inefficiently high taxation of immobile ones, such as non-tradable services. The structure of public expenditure may also be distorted, since location decisions are influenced by services received as well as by taxes paid. Competition for mobile capital may distort public spending towards items that benefit business (transport infrastructure) and away from those that benefit less mobile labour (social services). Regulations may benefit mobile factors at the expense of immobile factors (e.g. over-lax standards for reprocessing spent nuclear fuel).

To make the general point, consider this example in a little more detail. Acting non-cooperatively, each member state can compete for mobile capital in two ways: a lower tax on capital or a laxer ceiling on pollution. The result is an inefficiently low tax rate and an inefficiently high pollution level. Each state ignores the beneficial effects on others, in the form of an expanded tax base and a higher level of labour productivity, that would result if it were to raise its tax rate on capital and lower its maximum permitted pollution level. Even without direct pollution spillovers between member states, competition for mobile capital through reduced environmental standards yields an outcome in which all member states could gain from a coordinated raising of such standards.

4.3.2 Fiscal Competition and Distributional Equity

Fiscal competition inhibits redistributive policies. First, it appears efficient in each country to reduce taxes on mobile factors that were previously substantial net contributors to redistribution. In cutting tax rates, each country ignores the damage it does to other countries' tax bases and scope for redistribution through taxation. Second, to the extent there is intra-EC mobility of people (including new immigrants to the EC, whose mobility across EC countries may be higher than that of EC nationals), similar considerations apply to provision of public goods and welfare services. Neglecting the effects on other member states, each country has an incentive to retreat too far from the welfare state.

Together, these effects may have stark distributional implications for equity. For example, it appears that capital will go almost untaxed unless its taxation is centralized. (Since capital receives benefits from public goods, 'untaxed' does not imply a zero tax rate, but merely that taxes are no higher than benefits.) One might therefore expect owners of capital to extol the virtues of subsidiarity, while immobile people press hard either for the creation of centralized fiscal powers over capital taxation or the explicit coordination of national policies (an agreed floor to tax rates on capital). Monitoring the manner in which other countries apply capital taxation is far from easy; so in this particular example coordination of national policies lacks credibility. Concern over distribution would in this instance lead to centralization as the logical outcome.

Although we developed this basic point in relation to mobile capital, it applies to any factor that is sufficiently mobile within the EC and immobile across its external borders. Business executives and professional footballers tend to be mobile and high earners. Subsidiarity is likely to imply that they will therefore face low tax rates, which is surely not a distributional value judgement that would command wide support. Later in this chapter we consider the extent to which the entire view of the welfare state – the state as insurance agent and redistributor from rich to poor – can survive at the level of the nation state. To the extent that it cannot, one would again expect those who look forward to its demise to be the most vigorous advocates of subsidiarity and those keenest for its continuation to be the most avid supporters of fiscal centralization within the EC.

Thus far, this chapter has highlighted the problems that will arise if fiscal policy remains the responsibility of individual nation states within the EC. It may appear that our arguments lead to the natural conclusion that greater centralization is required. This issue is not so simple, however, as we now explain.

4.4 Accountability: The Argument Against Coordination at the EC Level

The principle of subsidiarity reminds us that centralization is prone to government failure. Even when decentralization has disadvantages, it is necessary to ask whether the disadvantages of centralization might not be greater.

A pervasive problem arises because of imperfect information. Central government finds it difficult to act in the best interests of its diverse citizens because it finds it hard to get access to the relevant information about them. The problem arises much less from any physical distance than from incentives to reveal or withhold information on which the centre depends. For example, the precise form of the collectively efficient intervention in the presence of fiscal externalities is likely to be very sensitive to details about consumer behaviour (and hence implicitly to consumers' valuations of the benefits of particular goods and services) and about producer behaviour (and the implicit costs of production), as formal theoretical analyses make clear. Thus, in the environmental standards case discussed above, the efficient outcome depends on each member state's marginal valuation of environmental improvements, a magnitude which is not easy to observe and one which member states may have incentives to misrepresent. Such imperfect information means that mistakes will be made in the formulation of a coordinated policy, whose costs may exceed the benefits of mitigating the externality in question. There is no reason to suppose that an efficient coordinated policy is one in which each member state adopts the same tax rates or the same environmental standards. It must also be recognized that the negotiation and enforcement of a coordinated policy intervention involves administrative costs. It is quite possible that the final outcome of coordination may be worse than non-cooperative behaviour by the individual member states.

Potentially the most important reason why coordination may be undesirable is that policy-makers may not be trying to represent the public interest in the first place. The 'public choice' approach to policy analysis emphasizes that we need a theory of government as much as a theory of private sector behaviour; policy decisions cannot automatically be assumed to reflect the pursuit of the public interest, however defined. Instead, politicians and bureaucrats, like consumers and firms, must be regarded as selfish agents pursuing their own interests, and subject to their own particular sets of constraints and pressures. For example, this view leads to the presumption of a systematic tendency for governments to set taxes inefficiently high, either because the rewards to policy-makers, both financially and in the enjoyment of power, increase with the size of their budgets, or because voting procedures may enable the formation of coalitions which bias decisions towards excessive expenditure. If this view of government is correct, coordination among member states in response to fiscal externalities involving each others' tax bases is undesirable. Any efficiency gain from internalizing this externality is outweighed by larger efficiency losses from the suppression of competition between non-cooperating jurisdictions, which acts as a brake on the central government's capacity to appropriate and waste resources, thereby bolstering the otherwise very inadequate political and constitutional constraints on governments. Such a view has been explicitly advocated in the context of EC tax developments by the UK government (HM Treasury, 1988).

Tax competition is thus to be welcomed, and coordination regretted, if one regards governments as acting entirely in their own interests, but these conclusions are exactly reversed if one regards governments as acting entirely in the public interest. Unfortunately, evidence that enables a choice to be made between these two views of government is hard to find, and the truth is almost certain to lie between these two extremes. Hence the question of whether any downward pressure on EC member states' tax revenues consequent on tax competition is to be welcomed or regretted is more than just a matter of the view taken of government: the quantitative extent of that revenue reduction is also important.

In analysing this problem of the conflicting pressures to centralize and decentralize, it is important to try to get beyond 'on the one hand, on the other hand' discussions, and it is possible do so (for further details, see Edwards and Keen, 1993). If we take the inefficiency of centralization seriously, we could think of putting a number on it. Suppose, for example, that 40% of marginal public expenditure is waste; the other 60% is not waste. If revenues fall by 1 ECU, there is a gain to the private sector of 0.4 ECU that would otherwise be wasted, but there is also a loss of 0.6 ECU of useful public expenditure. That public expenditure may be worth more or less than 0.6 ECU to the public; in a second-best world, it will usually be more, since the presence of distortions in tax collection means that valuable opportunities for public expenditure have been neglected.

Revenues under tax competition are more likely to be inefficiently low the more tax competition reduces revenue (the effect studied in Section

4.3) and the less wasteful is the government (the effect introduced in Section 4.4). The strength of the former effect will depend on the responsiveness of the tax base to tax differentials: tax competition will result in lower revenues the more mobile is the tax base between competing jurisdictions. Combining these two considerations, the question of whether tax competition in some area of tax policy is desirable can be resolved by comparing two numbers:

(a)the proportion of marginal public expenditure which is pure waste; and

(b)the elasticity of a jurisdiction's tax base with respect to the tax in question.

Tax competition is undesirable – more precisely, non-cooperative tax setting leads to rates that are too low for the collective good – if and only if the second of these numbers is larger than the first. Suppose, for instance, the elasticity is 0.3: then tax competition will be desirable if and only if more than 30% of marginal public expenditure is pure waste.

This simple rule does not resolve the different views about the costs and benefits of competition. In practice, it is hard to estimate the two critical quantities. The model of reality which underlies the rule is highly simplified: it assumes, for instance, that governments do not have any recourse to an immobile tax base. Nevertheless, the rule is useful in moving discussion on from an exchange of articles of faith about government behaviour towards matters capable of empirical resolution. Notice, in particular, that individuals may have widely divergent views on the nature of government and yet agree on the desirability or otherwise of tax competition. Suppose, for example, that the elasticity of the tax base is agreed to be 0.4. Then it does not matter whether one believes that 1% or 30% of marginal public expenditure is wasted: in either case, tax competition leads to inefficiently low tax rates.

One other aspect of this rule is worth noting. Since there is no reason to think that either of the two critical quantities has the same magnitude in all EC member states, it is possible that tax competition will be simultaneously good for some and bad for others. It may be, for example, that government expenditure is sufficiently wasteful for British citizens to benefit from intensified tax competition while pressures on revenue in Germany, say, would be undesirable.

Having developed a general framework in which to analyse factor mobility and fiscal competition, we now turn to specific applications.

4.5   Can Capital Income Taxes Survive?

EC countries currently use a mixture of residence- and source-based taxes on the income from capital. The most important source tax is the corporate tax on retained earnings, collected by the country in which the profits are generated and not the country where the owner resides and in which they accrue. The most important residence tax is the personal income tax on income from interest and dividends on capital assets. In theory it is applied by all OECD countries. In practice it is hard to administer, since foreign income can be hidden from domestic tax authorities. For a selection of countries, three inside the EC and three outside, Table 4.3 shows recent estimates of the tax revenue raised by taxation of profits and capital; the revenue raised through personal income taxes on both labour income and income from capital; and other principal sources of revenue. Table 4.3 shows that source-based taxes on capital income typically account for less than 10% of government revenue (though over 20% in Japan).

Source-based taxes on capital, or the income therefrom, are bound to be driven even lower by fiscal competition in a world of greatly-enhanced capital mobility between nation states, and Figure 4.1 confirms that this process has already begun. How low would unfettered fiscal competition drive such tax rates? Eventually, to the point at which the country's marginal social cost of hosting capital equals its marginal social benefit. In a second-best world where raising revenue through other taxes also causes distortions, the marginal benefit of 1 ECU of tax revenue will exceed 1 ECU (since distortions from raising alternative revenue can be

Table 4.3: Sources of Taxation. 1989. Percentage of Government Revenues.

Source	EC			Non-EC		
	UK	*Germany*	*France*	*Sweden*	*US*	*Japan*
Profits and Capital	12	5	7	5	9	21
Personal Incomes	27	26	14	40	38	23
Consumer Spending	43	30	35	30	27	28
Social Security	18	39	44	25	26	28

Source: UK Central Statistical Office, *Economic Trends*, January 1992.

avoided). The marginal cost is essentially the cost of hosting additional capital, for example the necessary public infrastructure for useful private investment. Unbridled tax competition with perfect capital mobility makes the corporate tax mutate towards a pure benefit tax in which what companies pay in any state is primarily related to the services they then enjoy.

The last two decades have seen a world-wide removal of barriers to capital mobility. One implication of this was shown in Figure 4.1. The average of the corporate tax rates of the G7 countries had declined significantly, from 45% in 1974 to 37% in 1993, and the reduction in the dispersion of tax rates is also striking, especially within the large countries of the EC. The change in both the average level and the dispersion may partly reflect a switch in political mood – greater reliance on market forces, less government intervention and less income redistribution – but it also reflects greater capital mobility and diminished scope for raising revenue through taxation of capital income, corroborating the market pressures behind our analysis. Indeed, as we shall shortly argue, the market pressures stemming from greater factor mobility may themselves be one of the underlying causes of the change in political mood.

A natural reaction to the difficulty in raising source taxes on capital is a switch to the residence principle of taxation, according to which residents pay tax regardless of where their capital is invested. There are practical difficulties (tax evasion) in implementing a true residence tax. More significantly, such a tax is not safe from tax competition. Instead of driving capital out of the country, it may expel the capital owners, and hence the tax base, whether or not they take their capital with them. If people were as mobile as capital, the outcome of such fiscal competition would be precisely the same as with a source tax: taxes driven down to levels equating social marginal benefit and cost in host countries, an outcome in which the taxation of capital is inefficiently low and compensated by some combination of inefficiently high taxes on less mobile factors and inefficiently low levels of the government spending that tax revenue finances. The source of these inefficiencies is the fiscal externalities discussed in Section 4.2. We accept that owners of capital are likely to be less mobile in the long run than capital itself; considerations of tax evasion aside, residence-based capital income taxes are therefore unlikely to be eroded to quite the same extent as source-based taxes. Nevertheless, Germany's current tax reform (the so-called residence securing law) shows concern about just such a possibility. Whichever system is in place, the erosion of capital income taxes in a Europe of fiscal competition is a safe prediction.

The erosion of capital income as a part of the general tax base clearly has important implications for income and wealth distribution, as we emphasized in Section 4.2. The immobile poor and disadvantaged will bear part of this burden in higher taxes and lower welfare provision. On pure efficiency grounds, however, the case is less clear-cut, because of two conflicting inefficiencies. Failure to internalize fiscal externalities is a source of inefficiency leading to undertaxation of mobile capital. There are strong arguments which suggest, however, that, even in a world of distortionary taxation, it is inefficient to tax marginal investments by firms. The starting-point may therefore have involved inefficiently high taxation of capital. Hence, given the types of taxation currently in place, the principal consequence of greater capital mobility may be the exacerbation of distributional inequity, not the creation of substantial new inefficiency.

Our preferred solution is to change the structure of taxation. Economists have long advocated replacing the capital income tax with a cash-flow tax like the Meade Committee's R-base or S-base taxes, or Sinn's (1987) mixed system. Cash-flow taxes are regularly levied taxes that act as once-and-for-all levies on the existing capital stock but exempt all future marginal investment (i.e. investments whose returns just cover their costs). Basically, they replace the right to depreciate existing assets with the right to deduct gross investment from the tax base. The cash-flow tax offers a solution to the problem of tax competition by reconciling the needs of efficiency, equity and accountability, at least in the short-to-medium run.

Capital that has been accumulated historically will be trapped and caught by the tax, while any new capital could freely migrate across the borders. Leaving new marginal investment untaxed meets the principal efficiency objective of not distorting firms' intertemporal choices through inefficiently high taxes. Intramarginal investments, which generate pure profits, are still taxed under the cash-flow system. The fact that intramarginal investments are still taxed means that the cash-flow tax does not wholly eliminate fiscal externalities through tax competition: for example, inward Japanese investment to the EC will typically generate pure profits, and the decision about which EC country to locate in will be affected by the rate at which such profits are taxed. Nevertheless, the addition of a cash-flow tax for companies will greatly reduce the problems of tax competition in a world of mobile capital.

Continuing to tax capital historically in place at rates similar to those that applied in the past prevents owners of existing capital from making windfall gains as a result of increased factor mobility; and it provides much-needed revenue for other objectives, including the provision of public goods and, perhaps, redistribution. And, by avoiding the need to centralize taxation of capital incomes, such cash-flow taxes make use of the principle of subsidiarity to pursue accountability through government at a lower level. While the details of a cash-flow tax system cannot be spelled out here, it is important to recognize that sensible alternatives to capital income taxation exist that survive the forces of tax competition and achieve these other benefits (see Sinn, 1987, for further discussion).

Is it credible for a government to announce that new capital will be untaxed? Surely once it is installed and becomes historical capital it will then be a sitting target for taxation. When investment is first undertaken, the government immediately allows full offset against tax liability of profits from other investment; subsequently this transfer is gradually clawed back as taxes on the future profits on the investment are earned. The incentive-compatible feature of the scheme is that the government contributes its part at the outset, on which it cannot subsequently renege. It could raise the tax rate over time, however, despite promising not to do so. This would have the consequence of taxing investment once it had been sunk into bricks and metal. Fear of such an eventuality might then cause investment to flee the country in the first place.

There appear two solutions to this danger. The first is EC-wide ceilings on such cash-flow taxes; the second is to rely on the repeated game character of the relationship between government and owners of capital. At any particular time, it may appear that the government has an incentive to cheat *ex post*. But, at that date, it will be dealing with new investors on an *ex ante* basis. They are likely to be scared off if they observe the government reneging on promises to their predecessors. In this respect, preservation of a large number of fiscal jurisdictions is important: it gives new investors, who are mobile within the EC, a credible threat to go somewhere else. In contrast, to the extent that capital is less mobile between the EC and the rest of the world, a promise by today's EC governments to coordinate a ceiling on the tax rate may offer a more limited guarantee that tax rates will not be raised in the future.

The principal alternative to our proposed cash-flow tax at the level of member states is centralization of capital income taxes in the hope of levying collectively a higher tax rate by internalizing fiscal externalities within the EC. Such an alternative may not only lead to a tax that is inefficiently high (by continuing to neglect the case for not taxing marginal investments by firms); it may also prove infeasible (since its efficacy rests on capital mobility within the EC being substantially greater than capital mobility across the EC's external frontiers). If the latter is also large, fiscal competition between the EC and other parts of the world will still drive tax rates down; it would take a global agreement to maintain higher tax rates. Such global agreements are not unknown – it is no accident that the Basel Agreement on prudential requirements for banks applies in the industry whose market is the most globally integrated – but they are usually hard to secure. It is a merit of our proposal for a cash-flow tax that, since new marginal investment is effectively untaxed and free to move, it requires no such global agreement.

4.6   Competing for VAT Revenue

Suppose for whichever of the reasons discussed above, the EC finds its tax revenue from capital income reduced. A likely candidate for replacing lost revenue is the value-added tax (VAT), which has functioned well in Europe and is free from the distortions created by the capital income tax because it exempts investment.

Unfortunately, however, VAT is not immune from tax competition. Until recently, the accumulated VAT incorporated in a product was rebated at the border when the product left the country of origin; and the country of destination imposed its own VAT instead. Europe had a destination-based VAT that itself left investment goods untaxed and undistorted. Things changed with the removal of border controls at the beginning of 1993. Unrestricted cross-border shopping is now allowed at the country of origin's VAT rate, moving the EC from a destination-based towards an origin-based VAT system. A full move towards an origin-based system may cause two kinds of reaction.

First, external trade confronts a small country with prices it must take as given: these will now apply to tax-inclusive rather than the net-of-tax prices of consumption in terms of investment goods. The pure consumption tax now starts to distort production decisions. It is one of the main messages of the optimal trade literature that a small country should try to avoid such a tax. Given this result, a general tendency to cut tax rates is to be expected.

Second, firms face strong incentives to avoid paying the high taxes by artificially shifting the tax base to low-tax countries. While the new tax rules allow for unrestricted cross-border shopping, they effectively adhere to the destination principle when commodities are traded among firms. The exporting firm continues to receive a full tax rebate, and the importing firm has to pay the full domestic tax. This enables firms in high-tax countries to serve their domestic customers by channelling their products through retailers in low-tax countries. Through this procedure the domestic tax can be fully replaced by the foreign tax. Competition for these tax bases may induce a fierce downward competition in tax rates. Countries will try to undercut their neighbours and attract as much retail business as they can. Thus the EC will face in product markets the same fiscal externalities that we analysed in Sections 4.2–4.4.

When transactions costs shrink, then in theory fiscal competition could drive VAT rates down towards the marginal social cost of hosting the retail business; yet VAT revenue is needed for many other purposes as well. Even though this is only the limiting case, and evidence for example from competition among individual states in the USA suggests we are not yet close to such a point, the general point is valid: the fiscal spillovers inflicted by competition for this tax base are significant and likely to increase over time. Not only is there a powerful case for coordinating VAT rates across member states, but the appropriate higher tier at which this should be done is clearly the level of the EC: unlike capital income taxes, where mobility across EC frontiers is a serious possibility, cross-border shopping and warehousing in Japan and the US are not major problems.

The EC appears to share much of this analysis. Already, it has imposed lower bounds on the national VAT rates. Since monitoring the treatment of VAT in other member states is relatively straightforward, this seems to us an appropriate reflection of the analysis of Chapter 3. Concerted action in this instance can credibly be undertaken through implementation at the national level of rules agreed by the EC as a whole. Centralization of the entire VAT system is not necessary, and decentralization provides the correct solution.

4.7 The Erosion of the Welfare State?

One central idea underlying a nation state is mutual assistance within its borders. In this respect, the nation state is an insurance state and a redistributive state. By agreeing on a system of fiscal redistribution from rich to poor, citizens do more than insure themselves against the risks of disease, missed opportunities, physical inabilities and the like; they also participate in systematic and foreseeable transfers, whose purpose is to mitigate the consequences not of future contingencies but of disparities in the current and essentially observable distribution of life chances.

Fiscal competition will put pressure on the welfare state, because the effects discussed in the cases of the capital income and value-added taxes will occur in similar forms with *all* taxes on mobile economic activities. As tax rates on mobile activities are driven down, active redistribution by taxing the rich and giving to the poor will become more difficult. In Section 4.4, we observed that in general this will affect the political economy of which groups tend to favour coordinated rather than decentralized approaches to the development of Europe. It is owners of mobile factors, probably those with physical and human capital, that will personally benefit most from decentralization. Immobile factors, including some types of labour but also the disadvantaged and the infirm, will tend to seek the protection that can be offered only by much greater coordination of national policies, some of which will require centralization but some of which need not. Whereas in Section 4.4 our interest was partly in the incentives to support a particular evolution of Europe, we now wish to focus in more detail on activities of the insurance state itself in such circumstances. (Subsequent chapters take up some related issues. Chapter 5 discusses how such arguments relate to 'Social Europe', while Chapter 6 discusses macroeconomic stablization of the aggregate economy.)

In the most extreme case, complete mobility would imply that altruism and charity remained the only reasons for redistribution. Undoubtedly, feelings of Frenchness, Germanness or Britishness remain important; concern for others with whom one identifies may be a significant determinant of behaviour. Moreover, as we stressed in Chapter 3, it is the package of taxes and public goods that matters to potentially mobile taxpayers, and the range of choice is sufficiently limited to provide significant inertia: people with cultural and family roots in a particular country may so like its ambience and its public goods (and over time the two may become connected) that their national government has some scope for raising taxes without automatically inducing them to leave. Similar economies of scope may lead workers with particular skills to cluster in particular localities; if Europe continues to specialize in this way, there may not be suitable jobs elsewhere to allow skilled workers to move to escape taxation. Having dismantled formal barriers to migration within the EC, it is on such inertia that the survival of the redistributive state at national level will depend. Although inertia may be sufficient to permit moderate redistribution between different types of factors that are not *de facto* very mobile, the feasible extent of redistribution within countries is curtailed by an increase in the mobility of factors, notably of capital and the most affluent workers. We can be sure of the direction of the change. The key issues are the extent (will labour mobility. remain limited?), and how much of this has already taken place (are capital taxes already low?). We try to answer these questions below.

We noted above that a well-functioning nation state might be defined as having boundaries within which citizens felt a mutual commitment and a willingness to participate in insurance and redistribution. When this commitment breaks down, separatist movements may emerge, as in Belgium and Italy. This points up a difficulty in the argument that centralization is needed when decentralization breaks down. Centralizing aspects of the insurance or welfare state would overcome those particular difficulties that arise from mobility among lower-level jurisdictions to avoid taxation or take advantage of generous welfare systems. But centralization may run into another difficulty, namely that people in the UK may be unwilling to contribute to support the poor in Greece, or people in Germany to support people in Portugal. When such problems arise, there will be a limit to the extent to which any form of coordination at EC level can mitigate the erosion, albeit partial, of the welfare state that will be inevitable under decentralization.

Yet since individuals are risk averse and face major risks in their own lives and in the lives of their descendants, pressure for the welfare state to re-emerge may be powerful: problems of moral hazard and adverse selection make it difficult to unfurl the umbrella of adequate insurance protection using private contracts; and some sense of underlying altruism and collective responsibility is likely to place a floor on the extent to which redistribution can comfortably be abandoned. Perhaps one day yet cheaper transport and communications will build links within Western Europe to the point at which a sufficiently common identity exists to enable the necessary coordination at EC level to place the safety of the welfare state beyond question. Until that day arrives, however, the analysis of this section suggests that the welfare state will remain under pressure. As we now show, however, this pressure is likely to grow for other reasons.

4.8   Old Age Pensions and Public Debt

The next problem we address is the stability of Europe's pay-as-you-go old age pension systems, which are 'unfunded'. Contributions by the young are not invested to pay later for their own old age; rather, their contributions today immediately finance the pensions of the previous generation. In a sense, state pensions resemble a 'chain letter', built on the assumption that the next generation of contributors will be numerous enough then to finance the pensions of today's generation. In fact, the growth rate of the contributions to the system is the implicit rate of return on social security saving.

Chain letters are inherently unstable contracts. If it is believed that few people will participate in the future, it does not pay to participate today; this belief is self-fulfilling. This instability has led the European countries to make participation in the public old age pension systems obligatory for large fractions of the labour force. A system from which people cannot withdraw, regardless of the implicit return the system offers on contributions, is one that will not face dramatic instability. Even so, citizens have found a way gradually to withdraw, by having fewer children. With an ageing demographic structure, it is already certain that substantial tax revenue from other sources will be needed within the next decade if nation states are to meet existing pension obligations (see e.g. Börsch-Supan, 1991).

Increased mobility in Europe will exacerbate this situation. Slowly growing countries offer low rates of return on social security investment, and they may therefore face emigration (of young potential investors in pensions) which reduces the growth rate even more. Again we concede that, for the time being, the immobility of large parts of respective national populations may contain this problem. With further integration, however, both economic and cultural (satellite TV is no respecter of national boundaries), intra-EC migration is likely to become easier, not more difficult. The problem can only get worse.

The risk of destabilizing migration applies not only through pensions but also through public debt and national indebtedness. Public debt is a claim on future taxpayers just like a pension claim. If people expect emigration, they know that the burden of the debt will have to be borne by fewer taxpayers, which provides a large incentive to escape by migration. Again the expectation is self-fulfilling and destabilizing. Since enhanced labour mobility is likely to be confined principally within the EC, in this case coordination at the EC level seems the appropriate solution. Effectively, this would mean either explicit centralization though federal fiscal policy and pension schemes or measures to organize policy that is coordinated centrally but carried out at the level of national governments.

The latter would mean that migration *per se* did not allow people to withdraw from fiscal and pension programmes with which they began. An Italian who emigrated to Denmark would still face tax liabilities and pension contributions in Italy, which would remove incentives to migrate for purely fiscal or pension incentives, while properly leaving open other incentives (e.g. higher productivity and pre-tax income, or preference for consumption of particular types of scenery).

Enforcement issues and administrative costs aside, such an institutional framework faces two potential problems. First, by divorcing taxation from residence (and hence consumption of public goods and the ability to observe government performance), it would diminish the accountability of national governments, a danger we take seriously. Second, by enshrining the 'nationality of origin principle' in taxation, it would tend to enhance nationalism at the very time when the market pressures of integration and mobility are inching the EC towards a continental identity, however slow this process may be. Thus, the nationality principle may offer respite for some time to come, especially if labour mobility is not yet extensive. Should the dynamics of pension schemes and government finances become precarious, however, the EC may sooner or later be driven to the only other possible solution – explicit centralization through fiscal federalism.

4.9 Conclusions

The basis of the principle of subsidiarity is the presumption that government failure at the centre remains of pressing concern. Pointing to potential deficiencies of fiscal competition is not in itself sufficient to legitimate the growth of a federal fiscal structure in Brussels that risks capture by rent-seekers and faces difficulties in remaining accountable to the citizens of the EC.

On the other hand, after carefully working through the fiscal issues that would arise from unfettered fiscal competition among member states against a background of enhanced mobility of products and factors, we are struck by the accuracy of our opening conjecture: fiscal business as usual will not remain a viable option indefinitely.

Europe's fiscal future cannot be built on the principle of exempting from the burden of financing public expenditure those who happen to be able to escape national tax collectors. Escape routes can be closed or at least curtailed. Accountability, distributive justice and economic efficiency require that action be taken. Where mobility of products or factors raises acute difficulties, the dangers of collective action are outweighed by the certain consequences of collective inaction. We have stressed that some so-called difficulties may not be acute, and decentralization may be the lesser evil. When we have diagnosed problems as acute, we have broadly followed the precept: 'decentralize where possible, coordinate where necessary, centralize only when that coordination would not be credible.'

And what of the questions posed at the outset? Can the nation state survive? Must the welfare state be eroded unless the EC now wholeheartedly embraces fiscal federalism?

We have certainly drawn attention to trends which, if continued, will be forces pressurizing the taxing powers of nation states and their ability to meet in full the aspirations of the welfare state. On the other hand, the Community has not yet reached the stage, and may never do so, at which it is faced with the starkest of choices: centralize or watch the welfare state wither away. What considerations lie behind this assessment that the position is not yet precarious?

First, in Section 4.1 we presented evidence that casts some doubt on the extent of labour mobility, not only within the EC but even in small countries such as Switzerland. Although labour mobility will increase within the EC, it is unlikely to do so quickly, unless the EC admits large numbers of legal immigrants from the East. In the mean time, broadly based taxes on workers' income and spending will furnish governments with substantial revenue even if these gradually become harder and harder to raise. Second, although we have little doubt that capital mobility within the EC is high, it is precisely *because* it is already high that some of the Doomsday effects have already taken place. Figure 4.1 shows that corporate tax rates have already fallen substantially; so have the highest marginal rates of personal income tax. Table 4.3 confirms that already EC member states do not raise significant revenue from taxation of capital income. Third, some of the most obvious channels of fiscal competition are already being blocked, as for example in the floor imposed on VAT rates within the EC.

If this assessment is correct, it is certainly a viable fiscal option for the Community to remain primarily a confederation of nation states.[1] In such a world, the welfare state will survive, perhaps at a diminished level and certainly under perpetual scrutiny. Redistribution will occur, and it will increasingly be based on redistribution of labour income; highly mobile capital will make even less contribution than it makes today. And the threat of potential labour mobility will skew the forms that redistribution then takes. High marginal tax rates will be hard to sustain. Redistribution within the richer half of the population is likely to become minimal. Rather, what will survive are broadly based taxes which enable some provision, increasingly selectively targeted, to be made for the poorer citizens of each member state.

It is a vision that fits quite appropriately the limited social objectives of the parties of the right, who should be expected to espouse this framework with enthusiasm, and a vision that straitjackets the much greater social ambitions of the left, who should be expected to reject such a framework out of hand.

Note

[1] These states are likely, however, to wish to agree a common policy on legal immigration from outside the EC, and perhaps even to harmonize the entitlements to benefits of those admitted to EC countries on political or humanitarian grounds, during the transitional period before they become full citizens of EC member states.

5   Social Europe, Social Dumping and Subsidiarity

In this chapter, we discuss the design and implementation of social policies in Europe. The debate surrounding the Social Chapter of the Maastricht Treaty and the opt-out clause granted to the UK has placed at the forefront of debate the main issue we address here. Can social policies continue to be implemented at the national level? Or is social dumping inevitable in the absence of a common social policy? The principles elaborated in Chapters 3 and 4 have direct bearing on these questions.

By 'social' policies, we understand a broad range of collective actions taken to protect workers in the areas of working schedules (length of the work week, restrictions on overtime and night work, duration of paid vacations, age for mandatory retirement), hygiene and safety at work and working conditions in general, unemployment compensation and protection against layoffs and dismissals, and a minimum wage.

5.1   Diverse Social Arrangements ...

With the exception of minimum wage legislation which we address separately, one can think of all these actions, measures or pieces of legislation as helping to define the characteristics of a job and/or the form taken by the remuneration package attached to it. For both employer and employee, a job is defined not only by the tasks to be performed and the qualifications required but also by the daily work schedule, the number of working hours in a week or a year, and the safety, health and comfort conditions under which the tasks are performed. All affect both the disutility of work for the employee and the output an employer obtains from a worker net of what must be spent on providing adequate working conditions. Similarly, the worker's compensation for the services performed is typically a package with

Table 5.1: Expenditure on Social Protection in the EC. 1989.

	Total Protection		Composition of Protection: % paid by		
	% of GDPper Resident	Amount	Employers	Employees	Government
Belgium	27	4,026	41	27	29
Germany	27	4,551	40	31	26
Denmark	30	4,347	9	5	80
Spain	17	2,054	53	19	26
France	28	4,451	52	29	17
Greece	16	1,198	–	–	–
Italy	23	3,572	53	15	30
Ireland	21	2,004	24	15	60
Luxembourg	26	5,153	33	23	38
Netherlands	30	4,644	31	35	17
Portugal	18	1,320	49	19	27
UK	21	3,173	–	–	–
EC(12)	25	3,574	42	24	28

Source: *Eurostat.*
Notes: Amounts per resident are measured in Purchasing Power Standards (in 1985 ECU); data for Greece, UK, and EC(12) are estimates.

many components: not only a direct wage but also indirect payments such as the employer's contributions for health insurance and retirement, payments in kind and the right to paid leave for vacations or sickness. The length of the contract and the probability of its renewal or termination (or implicit commitment to lifetime employment) are also relevant elements of the compensation package.

Before asking why the nature of the contract signed by a worker and an employer is typically restricted by law or industry convention, and whether it should be, we note the remarkable diversity of current social

Table 5.2: Structure of Labour Costs of Industrial Workers.
1988. Percentage of Total Labour Cost.

	Direct Labour Cost		Indirect Labour Cost	
	Salary	*Bonuses*	*Social Security*	*Other*
Belgium	49	20	29	2
Denmark	83	13	3	1
Germany	56	20	22	2
Greece	61	19	19	1
Spain	55	20	24	1
France	51	17	29	3
Ireland	70	12	15	3
Italy	50	20	27	3
Luxembourg	68	15	16	1
Netherlands	55	18	24	3
Portugal	56	18	22	4
UK	85	1	12	2

Source: *Eurostat.*

arrangements in the EC member states. Table 5.1 shows wide differences in relative and absolute levels of social expenditures in the EC. As a percentage of GDP, the Netherlands spends nearly twice as much as Greece, and in absolute terms differences are wider still. There is also substantial variation in how such expenditure is financed: state contributions as a percentage of total receipts vary from 17% to 80%, employers contributions from 9% to 35%, individuals' contributions from 5% to 35%. It is not surprising to see as a result that the structure of labour costs, or the form taken by the typical compensation package, varies similarly (see Table 5.2).

Table 5.3 provides evidence on other dimensions of the job characteristics or compensation package: paid vacations, sickness and maternity leaves, the length of the work week and total annual work

Table 5.3: Paid Vacations, Sickness and Maternity Leave, Length of Work Week and Annual Work Time. 1986.

	Vacation (Weeks)		Sickness Leave		Maternity Leave		Work Week (Hours)		Annual Work Time
	L	C	Weeks	B%	Weeks	B%	L	C	Hours
Belgium	4	4–5	52	60	14	80	40	36–40	–
Denmark	–	5	91	90	28	90	–	37.5–40	1,733
Germany	3	5.5–6	78	80	14	100	48	37.5–40	1,697
Spain	4	4.5–5	8–26	60–75	16	75	40	37–40	1,800
France	5	5–6	52	50–67	16	84	39	35–40	1,767
Greece	4	4	26	50	15	50	41	35–40	–
Ireland	3	4	52	75	14	70	48	35–40	1,864
Italy	–	4–6	26	50–67	20	80	48	36–40	1,768
Luxembourg	5	3.5–4	52	100	16	100	40	37–40	–
Netherlands	3	4–5	52	70	12	100	48	36–40	1,756
Portugal	4	4.5–5	155	65	13	100	48	34–38	2,025
UK	–	4–6	28	52–70	40	–	–	35–40	1,778

Sources: Institut Syndical Européen; Liaisons Sociales; EC.
Notes: Conventional = C, Legal = L, and Benefit relative to salary = B. Data for hours per annum are for 1988.

time. Further inquiry would show similar disparities in the generosity and the organization of unemployment insurance systems, wage bargaining structures, and the institutional levels at which regulatory measures are legislated and implemented. An illustration of the latter point is given by minimum wage regulations that we describe below (see Table 5.4 and the surrounding discussion below). Regulations of firing practices are similarly disparate although tedious to detail here; but to illustrate, there is no legal requirement in Italy or Portugal, and elsewhere the length of required notice period ranges from one week in the UK and Ireland (for workers less than two years in post) to 24 months in Greece (for workers with more than 28 years of service).

5.2   ...To be Harmonized?

The diversity of current labour market arrangements in the Community can be understood as the result of a slow historical process. While the common starting-point can plausibly be traced to the industrial revolution, which made clear the necessity for collective action in the area of workers' protection, the particular form taken by public intervention in a given country is attributable to specific cultural factors, its industrial mix (since risk characteristics of jobs differ across industries), level of economic development (safety is certainly a normal good and probably a luxury good), and idiosyncrasies of bargaining processes (labour market institutions differ from country to country). The diversity of the national solutions adopted to resolve a common problem is *prima-facie* evidence in favour of a decentralized organization of social policies, in the absence of overriding motives for centralization.

Yet European texts, from the Treaty of Rome onwards, tend to suggest that the next stage in this historical process must be one of convergence of social systems across the Community. While the Treaty asserts that the natural functioning of the common market will 'favour the harmonization of social systems' (Article 117), the Single European Act is more explicit in asserting the member states' 'objective [of] harmonization of conditions .. especially in the working environment, as regards the health and safety of workers' and in providing competence to the Council to 'adopt, by means of directives, minimum requirements for gradual implementation, having regard to the conditions and technical rules obtaining in each of the Member States' (Article 118A). The validity of the decision process is reiterated in the Protocol on Social Policy annexed to the Maastricht Treaty, which also spells out the areas for which a unanimous decision of the Council is required. In accord with these texts, the Community has adopted a large number of detailed directives setting up minimum standards (to become effective over time) especially in the areas of health and safety in the work-place.

Does the process of closer European integration and increasing factor mobility indeed make inevitable the adoption of a common social policy, whether by complete harmonization of social systems or acceptance of common minimum standards? Or can differences in national preferences for social interventions continue to be implemented efficiently at the national level? These are the main questions we address in the present chapter. As an appetizer, let us observe that any concept of social dumping clearly presupposes the presence of spillovers between individual economies which provides one argument for coordination at EC level to set against subsidiarity and the underlying presumption that government failures at EC level are typically the greater concern.

5.3 Social Spillovers in Well-functioning Labour Markets?

To clarify the issue, we start by analysing the case of efficiency-motivated regulatory measures in an economy with properly functioning labour markets. We thereafter study deviations from this bench-mark.

There are three reasons to regulate the nature of the contracts between workers and employers: asymmetric information, externalities and time inconsistency. The first refers to the difficulty for workers in gathering information on the exact characteristics of both the jobs they are offered and the compensation packages attached to them. It may be difficult for a worker to evaluate *ex ante* the precise nature and extent of the risks to health and safety a proposed job entails; the fine print in a contract, which specifies rights under all sorts of contingencies, is equally difficult to assess. Regulatory provision for imposed minimum standards helps reduce the cost of, and need for, information gathering by workers, and it limits the potential for abuse on the part of better-informed employers (who otherwise might make deceptively attractive job offers, including for example high wages but low safety on the job, whenever the latter is difficult for others to estimate). This makes labour markets more transparent, making prices more efficient signals of scarcity and reward, and it therefore also makes then more competitive.

Second, whenever health and safety are concerned there is an externality linked to national health-care systems. In case of accident or illness, neither the employer nor the worker bears the full cost of treatment. Consequently one cannot expect the full social cost to be internalized in their relation. In consequence, firms provide lower safety standards than is socially efficient.

Regulatory intervention, in this case the social protection of workers, drives a wedge between the cost of labour to the employer and the marginal value of holding the job for the worker. This is because the regulatory measure will be binding only for those firms for which the cost of the required investment, say in safety equipment, exceeds the capitalized value of marginal benefits current and future workers get from the extra safety. Otherwise, it would have been profitable to install the equipment the first place. The wedge ideally should correspond to the value of the externality imposed on the health system or to the gains in information gathering made possible by the regulation. It is intended to correct a market failure.

As with all taxes or interventions, the incidence of the regulations falls on both parties, suppliers and demanders, unless the supply of labour is inelastic, in which case the cost is borne exclusively by workers in the form of lower direct wages. This last possibility should be taken seriously. With hindsight we can confirm for the Common Agricultural Policy the prediction that simple economic theory made in advance: subsidies were primarily capitalized into land prices benefiting the owners of land and not the incomes of farm operators.

Thus, if social protection is provided for workers – and perhaps it is the least mobile workers for whom such protection is typically most important – we may obtain the paradoxical outcome that well-designed regulation potentially increases efficiency for the economy as a whole, but benefits least the group that the intervention was designed to help most because it drives down the wages of immobile workers. The gains accrue rather as lower taxes for quite different groups, not least employers and owners of firms. Of course, a government aware of the distinction between the nominal and ultimate incidence of its measures –

if such a government exists – can always compensate: having secured an efficiency gain which overcomes a market failure through regulatory intervention, it can then engage in further redistribution to undo the distributive as opposed to the efficiency consequences of its intervention.

The third efficiency-based reason for regulating labour market contracts is time inconsistency. New employees have to invest in learning how a firm works, training in the skills it requires, and acquiring 'firm-specific' human capital. Once it has been acquired, there is a temptation for employers not to reward the workers appropriately. Since the human capital is firm specific, the worker has no credible threat to go elsewhere. Regulations, for example on the circumstances and terms of redundancy, may be a useful commitment mechanism that allows the worker to embrace wholeheartedly the acquisition of firm-specific human capital, a good outcome for both firm and worker who can then divide the surplus from this profitable relationship.

Where social protection is intended to enhance efficiency by addressing market failures, increasing international competition has no first-order impact on the level of regulation. The increased degree of competition does not affect the value of the externality (the cost that dangerous or unhealthy jobs impose on the health system); nor does it affect either the value of making national labour markets more transparent or the need for suitable precommitments. Mobile capital will tend to move where labour costs are lower and this may be put pressure on some categories of wages, but if the level of regulation is optimal in the first place there is no direct reason for it to be altered. In this sense, there is no reason to fear social dumping in our bench-mark case. There are no spillovers in social policies.

5.4 The Second-best, Fiscal Competition and Social Dumping

Notice in the above analysis the interaction of the implicit assumptions about labour and capital mobility. If protected labour is very immobile, the ultimate incidence of some forms of social protection falls on workers in the sense that better working conditions are offset by lower wages, leaving the value of the package to the worker unaltered. Since it is also unaltered to the employer, it does not have any implications for capital mobility.

However, the more mobile are the categories of labour to which social protection applies, the more two other things happen. First, the entire incidence of social protection no longer falls on wages: instead, the value of the labour package to workers is raised and with it the cost of the labour package to the firm. Second, and in consequence, fiscal competition will tend to lead to underprovision of social protection in order to attract highly mobile capital in a second-best world in which taxation imposes distortions and governments compete for tax bases precisely because they think this allows them then to reduce tax-induced distortions; yet, because governments act non-cooperatively, such behaviour increases inefficiency.

Whether this constitutes a powerful demonstration that inadequate labour protection – social dumping – is the likely outcome depends rather on the motive for the regulation in the first place. For example, if the principal motive for regulating contracts is to provide a commitment mechanism that firms otherwise could not devise on their own, firms are major beneficiaries of such regulation: without it, workers will anticipate that investment in firm-specific capital will not subsequently be rewarded by employers and simply refuse to invest in it in the first place – hardly a recipe for a flood of inward investment. We conclude that this motive for social protection is unlikely to lead to social dumping.

The other two motives might offer some opportunities for luring mobile capital via fiscal competition. Over-lax safety standards certainly help employers and implicitly tax less mobile labour. Ignoring externalities imposed on national health systems has similar effects: the less mobile factors will bear the ultimate incidence in higher taxes or lower health care.

However, three considerations make us doubt whether social dumping is likely on any significant scale. First, to the extent that social protection assists firms and owners of capital (the precommitment motive), it will not lead to inefficiently low levels of protection. Second, precisely because capital is highly mobile, it already confers little social profit to a country seeking to entice it: the public goods which it demands are nearly as expensive as the tax revenue it confers. It is only the second-best circumstances, in which tax revenue is worth more than its face value because it then allows other distortionary taxes to be avoided, that provide any motive to solicit capital inflows. On balance, therefore, we find the arguments so far adduced to be unpersuasive as a rationale for substantial social dumping. Third, the level of social protection may have been inefficiently high in the first place, for reasons that we consider below. If so, downward pressure on social protection is a move towards efficiency not a move away from it, despite the fact that the particular groups that then lose out will try to portray it otherwise.

5.5 Minimum Wages and Social Competition

Measures for workers' protection are often justified on the grounds that they protect the unskilled, the underprivileged and the poor, and hence are a desirable form of redistribution. To the extent that such equity considerations lead to regulatory measures acting like a tax, as in the previous section, and that such a tax is optimally set in light of national preferences for equity, our analysis is unchanged. If, however, the effect of the regulation is to prevent labour markets from clearing, as is obviously the case with minimum wage legislation, our previous analysis has to be amended.

Five EC countries have nationally legislated minimum wages (France, Luxembourg, the Netherlands, Portugal and Spain); five others have minimum wages determined by collective bargaining at the national level (Belgium and Greece) or sectoral level (Denmark, Germany and Italy). Two (the UK and Ireland) have no legislated minimum wage. Table 5.4 provides data on the relative value of the minimum wage in the five countries with nationally-legislated minimum wages. At whatever level

Table 5.4: Minimum Wages in EC Countries with National Legislation.

	Age of Eligibility for Full Minimum Wage	*Minimum Wage as % of Average Gross Wage*
Spain	18	39
France	18	42
Luxembourg	18	36 (qualified workers)
		30 (unqualified workers)
Netherlands	23	58
Portugal	20	61 (industry and services)
		51 (domestic staff)

Note: Percentages are computed for 1990 average gross wages except for France and Luxembourg, which are computed from 1989 data.

Source: *Eurostat.*

they are decided, such measures should be the result of balancing equity gains with efficiency losses, particularly in the form of unemployment among less qualified workers. In principle, the terms of this trade-off are altered when capital is more mobile and fiscal competition fiercer: in terms of employment, a given equity benefit may then be costlier to achieve.

Even if minimum wages are not a particularly efficient redistribution mechanism at the national level, policy at the EC level may improve the efficiency-equity trade-off. Indeed, a little reflection shows that the problem is not so much due to minimum wages as to differences in wage levels independently of the existence of minimum wage legislation. It does not make sense to prescribe a common absolute minimum wage for both France and Portugal. Yet the fact that in relative terms, the minimum wage in Portugal in higher than in France for workers older than 20 (48% of the average wage in Portugal against 42% in France) is no consolation to the reality that industries intensive in low-skilled labour have an advantage in locating in Portugal. That is what economic integration is about.

Not only is it hard to see what a common policy on this matter could achieve that would not be in clear contradiction with the logic of European integration, but EC standards for a minimum wage would not even achieve its avowed objective: it would in fact protect poor workers in rich countries (e.g. unskilled workers in Denmark and France) at the expense of poor workers in poor countries (e.g. Greece and Portugal), which is hardly redistribution at the EC level. Thus, while economic integration is likely to worsen the efficiency-equity trade-off faced by national governments (yet another aspect of the erosion of the welfare state), centralizing minimum wage legislation is certainly not the answer.

5.6 Market Power and the Erosion of Labour Market Rents

Our picture of well-functioning labour markets is hard to reconcile with the reality of 20 years of high unemployment in Europe. The recent literature has proposed several explanations for the persistence of wage rates above equilibrium levels: powerful trade unions, insider-outsider distinctions, and efficiency-wage incentives to make the work force more accountable to its employers. The first two are relevant for the problem at hand: the power of trade unions or insiders applies to all dimensions of a worker's compensation package. In fact, to the extent that the non-wage dimensions of this package are less visible than the purely monetary dimension, the monopoly power of insiders may even tilt the worker's compensation towards these less visible dimensions, since the distortion they impose in the presence of high unemployment is less obvious.

If one accepts the view that labour market equilibria are affected by the market power of trade unions or insiders, a higher degree of European integration is likely to have an extra efficiency effect: it will tend to erode the power of insiders or trade unions. The main channel for this effect will probably not be through labour mobility itself. The source of insider power, by definition, tends to be location specific; and potentially the most mobile group, recent immigrants, are outsiders in every sense. Rather, insider power is undermined by greater mobility of goods, causing greater product market competition to bid away the surplus revenues that insiders have traditionally appropriated for themselves; and by greater capital mobility. Firms will have incentives to relocate wherever the power of insiders or trade unions, and hence the rent they extract, is smallest.

Given this diagnosis, further EC integration may indeed be accompanied by complaints of 'social dumping', as social provisions are reduced by national governments or employers responding to the weaker bargaining position of unions. But what is occurring is a removal of previous excessive levels of social protection. By eroding the power of insiders and unions, increased integration promotes efficiency and employment. A misguided attempt to defend this aspect of Social Europe would undermine one of the main benefits of integration.

The traditional rhetoric of industrial relations does not of course accord with the above description of labour markets. The traditional view emphasizes market power not of the workers but of the employers. Social intervention by the state is needed to protect workers from being exploited by capitalists who, because of their monopsony power, can pay workers less than their marginal product. Public intervention, in the form of safety standards, minimum wages and the like, is a second-best response in situations where the first-best response cannot be adopted.

The first-best response is to tackle directly the source of the problem, which in this case is assumed to be the power of incumbent employers. Entry of new employers, competition between firms, and consequent dilution of the power of individual employers is that remedy. If barriers to entry in national economies prevent that entry and competition from taking place at the level of the nation state, market integration at a higher level is precisely the first-best solution. It is good for workers who face the prospects of increasing compensation, both because of the gains from trade and thanks to the reduction of employers' monopsony power. Capital will go wherever workers are most exploited where it will compete for cheap labour services, bid up wages, and reduce the extent of exploitation.

By the same token, capital and goods mobility threatens the employers' rents and presumably would be forcefully opposed by them. This traditional view is hard to reconcile with high and persistent unemployment (it does not explain why employers do not choose a point on the labour supply curve) and with the strong and general support to the process of European integration given by employers' organizations. In any case, the exploitation view does not provide a stronger platform for a common social policy.

To sum up, we find no reasons to believe that the process of economic integration will undermine the ability of individual member states to make optimal decisions on social and health regulations in accord with their national preferences. If such regulations have been set too high or too low due to dysfunctional national labour markets, the integration process will help by decreasing the market power of unions, insiders or employers as the case may be and it will erode the associated rents. There is thus no case for centralizing or even coordinating social policies. The Social Chapter of the Maastricht Treaty is in fact in direct contradiction with the subsidiarity principle that the same Treaty espouses.

5.7 Dumping the Social Chapter

Our message is clear. It is likely to be politically unpalatable for two reasons at least. First, the pressure in favour of a common European social policy sometimes seems to originate in the perception that the process and the benefits of European integration have been thus far mostly in the hands of Corporate Europe and that countervailing actions are needed. The rhetoric often suggests that Europe will be social and have a common social policy or that it will be 'anti-social' if it has no such policy. Our arguing against the Social Chapter is likely to be read as siding with Corporate Europe and against 'social' forces. We can only reiterate that, in our view, the absence of a social policy at the European level is fully consistent with even the most extravagant national preferences for social protection.

Second, as in other chapters of this Report, we must face the fact that European integration may have distributional consequences, in this instance consequences unfavourable to groups in a position to form strong coalitions. For one thing, increasing competition from the Mediterranean countries of Europe clearly means downward pressure at the lower end of the salary scale in the richer member states. This pressure may be accompanied with a downsizing of the social cushion in industries where it used to be well above minimum standards. In addition, reduced insider or union power may also be accompanied by reduced benefits, including potentially a reduction of minimum standards in those countries and areas where they reflected rents rather than true national preferences.

One may expect, indeed one already observes, that labour organizations in the richer countries, confronted with workers losing some of their acquired rights, will not stand still; and they will find public support. Social dumping is a fearsome rallying cry! Furthermore, because fighting social dumping may often mean lessening the threat posed by existing and future competition in low-wage countries, corporate Northern Europe is likely to join the coalition. This danger should not be ignored. A constructive solution is likely to involve compensatory measures aimed at lessening the impact and providing alternative opportunities, for example by further efforts in the area of education and training or by measures reducing social security charges on unskilled labour (for a call in that direction, see Drèze and Malinvaud, 1993). For symbolic purposes, it might be useful in this particular instance to coordinate such policies at the European level.

6   Fiscal Policy and Macroeconomic Stabilization

In this chapter we consider the role of fiscal policy in macroeconomic stabilization. To date, the EC has neither developed nor planned to develop any such role at the Community level. The Maastricht Treaty is not about establishing a federal fiscal policy and places restrictions on the fiscal choices of member states (ceilings for government debt and deficits) only in order to safeguard the proposals for a common monetary policy at EC level.

Thus, member states retain the power of setting their fiscal policies; yet the need for, and macroeconomic effectiveness of, national fiscal policy is enhanced by monetary union. Without a national monetary policy, a member state experiencing a shock not affecting the rest of the EC has more need of its own fiscal policy for stabilization policy. Moreover, with interest rates subject to market forces at Community not national level, fiscal policy in a particular country will be less undermined by 'crowding out' through induced effects on interest and exchange rates.

It thus appears that, with regard to fiscal policy and macroeconomic stabilization, to date the principle of subsidiarity has been rigorously applied. In this chapter, we ask whether the current assignment of macroeconomic fiscal policy to national governments is indeed appropriate. We examine several possible arguments for greater centralization but conclude that such a case is difficult to make. The balance of economic argument continues clearly to favour the conduct of stabilization policy primarily at the level of nation states. If, at some future date, political considerations make it necessary to press ahead with fiscal integration, our analysis may also be used to indicate where there is some scope for transferring fiscal programmes to the Community without undue economic damage.

6.1 Insurance versus Borrowing

When subject to an adverse shock (for example a fall in demand, or a deterioration in supply and competitiveness), what can a country do? Under flexible exchange rates, the country could cut interest rates and the market would induce an exchange rate depreciation. Both would provide some relief. This channel is closed in a monetary union. What is left is what every individual can do: hope to have taken out insurance in advance, or borrow until things improve.

It is important to distinguish between temporary and permanent shocks. Initially we assume that shocks are temporary. Community-level fiscal stabilization amounts to an insurance contract for each member state. In return for paying to the EC part of the extra income arising from unexpectedly favourable disturbances, a country receives part its income shortfall following an adverse shock. With sufficient parties to the deal, not all facing the same shock at the same time, the EC can diversify some of the country-specific risk, providing insurance protection at little cost.

For a country faced with an adverse disturbance, the alternative is to borrow on international markets the equivalent of its shortfall, and to pay back later when incomes are unexpectedly high. This is what uninsured individuals would want to do. The government should do it on behalf of those who have less favourable access to credit than the government does. In that case, there is no need for Community-level intervention; fiscal policies are fully decentralized.

When is insurance better than borrowing? First, insurance reduces uncertainty: paying a known premium provides coverage in case of adverse occurrences. As we shall see, this advantage is mitigated by a number of qualifications, discussed shortly. Second, it is not always possible to borrow as much as is needed to offset completely the loss imposed by bad luck. Indeed, most individuals face a credit ceiling, not least because they may be unable to offer the resources of their descendants as collateral. Governments can; that is one reason that they usually face less difficulty in borrowing.

When shocks are permanent, things are very different. A country facing a permanent adverse shock is permanently worse off. This substantially undermines the case for borrowing to smooth out consumption: consumption needs to fall and remain permanently lower. The only borrowing that may be justified is that with which to finance investment in the once-off reallocation and retraining of resources to which the shock may give rise: such borrowing then spreads the adjustment burden appropriately across current and future generations rather than imposing all the costs of adjustment on those alive when the permanent shock occurs.

It is tempting to make a clean distinction. A succession of temporary shocks can be handled primarily through borrowing and reliance on the law of large numbers to smooth their average effect. In contrast, the capital markets offer very limited assistance in coping with permanent shocks to which the principal response should be a permanent change in consumption. Relative to borrowing, insurance offers at best minimal gains for handling temporary shocks, but *ex ante* it makes a substantial difference for permanent shocks. A country insured against permanent shocks is now substantially more secure precisely because the consequences of such shocks cannot be dissipated *ex post* through the capital markets.

Unfortunately the force of this distinction is not as great as it first appears for two reasons. First, even supposedly temporary shocks may have permanent consequences (hysteresis). For example, a temporary shock to this year's rate of return will affect the capital with which next year begins. Such shock propogation mechanisms then undermine the equivalence of insurance and borrowing even when the shocks themselves are temporary. Second, when shocks are permanent, the credibility of the promises of the mutual insurance club to keep paying out for ever to an unlucky member cannot be taken for granted. We return to this issue shortly. Here we merely note that the advantage of

Table 6.1: Estimates of Percentage of Stabilization Provided by Central Government.

France	Germany	US	Canada
–	–	30	17
37	42	17	–

Note: The degree of stabilization is the proportion of income loss which is compensated by the centre through consequently higher transfers or lower obligations.
Sources: Top row from Bayoumi and Masson (1993). Bottom row from Italianer and Pisani-Ferry (1992).

insurance over borrowing in handling permanent shocks is clearly less than it first appears.

At this juncture in the argument it may be useful to quantify the extent of insurance that extant federations appear to offer. It appears to be substantial. A representative sample of the many investigations of this question is presented in Table 6.1. Estimates are very uncertain, yet, taking France as bench-mark of a centralized state, it appears that the US and Canadian federations do less and the German federation does more stabilization. Both the US and Canada still provide a very significant amount of insurance.

There remains the possibility that borrowing by local government or private insurance provides the bulk of stabilization. In the case of the US, local constitutions prevent most states from running budget deficits and accumulating debts, in effect prohibiting countercyclical fiscal policies (for evidence, see Eichengreen, 1990). In Switzerland, cantons are in principle free to set their budgets as they please. Yet, in practice they operate under federal supervision and there is no reported case of reckless behaviour. This may be *prima-facie* evidence that private borrowing can stand the remainder of the strain.

Neither centralized nor federal states provide full insurance through centralized fiscal stabilization. There may be good reasons. Insurance schemes are known to suffer from a number of serious defects. Could these shortcomings become overwhelming when applied to sovereign states?

6.2 Moral Hazard

There are two ways in which Community insurance may elicit perverse national responses because of the phenomenon of 'moral hazard': a change in behaviour induced by the very act of taking out insurance that, being behaviour hard to monitor, cannot be precluded by the insurance contract itself. First, macroeconomic shocks may be self-inflicted wounds. It may be tempting to provoke a shock in order to claim EC resources (e.g. unrealistic wage claims by organized labour; the example of the ex-GDR is hard to forget). If excessive wage settlements provoke a recession, transfers from the rest of the Community would be triggered by a centralized scheme. In existing federations, this risk is limited because unions mostly operate at national level and thus internalize the costs of such behaviour. This is not the case in the EC, and it is unlikely to be so for a long time. A second example is that of excessive consumption. If productive investments are reduced because of insufficient saving, a country may end up facing a protracted recession, bordering on economic decline. If EC insurance covers the eventual shortfall in income and spending, a country could literally have its cake and eat it; or more accurately eat its own cake, and then eat another one supplied by the EC.

Traditional insurance contracts combat moral hazard by imposing deductibles: by making each insured person pay for a significant part of the cost, deductibles substantially reduce the incentive for self-inflicted wounds. This may one reason for the *partial* stabilization evident in Table 6.1.

Another risk with Community insurance is that, even if shocks are truly *bona fide*, the ease and speed at which they are absorbed depend on a number of characteristics that are under national control. The list of measures which deepen business cycles is large and well known; indeed,

Table 6.2: Switzerland: Canton-level Unemployment Benefits. Maximum Local Contribution as Percentage of Federal Benefits. February 1993.

Canton	*%*	*Canton*	*%*
Basel	100	Schaffhausen	80–90
Basel City	100	Soluthurn	90
Bern	90–150	Thurgau	90
Geneva	50–100	Ticino	80
Glaris	100	Uri	90
Jura	90	Vaud	100
Lucern	80	Zug	85
St Gall	90	Zürich	80–90

Source: Office fédéral de l'industrie, des arts et métiers et du travail, Bern.

much effort has gone in recent years into supply-side policies designed to identify and eliminate such features. The difficulty with supply-side policies is that they are painful in the short run and only bring rewards in the long run. Community insurance would turn this trade-off on its head: anti-supply-side policies would be rewarded in the short run yet insured in the long run.

A couple of examples reveal the seriousness of this issue. Unemployment insurance discourages labour mobility across skills, industries and regions. In the short run, it is popular. In the longer run, it raises equilibrium unemployment. Even so, it is politically extremely difficult to roll back excessively generous unemployment benefits. If the cost to the budget is borne at the EC level, each member state may have incentives to press for greater generosity still, whatever its aggregate impact on the EC. Another example is that of retraining programmes. They are known be an efficient way of shortening unemployment spells, but they cost money. Skimping on them would reduce national public spending and therefore taxes while eliciting EC transfers.

The response of existing federations seems to be to homogenize those features which affect the responsiveness to shocks. Thus, in Germany and Switzerland, unemployment schemes are set at the federal level. Yet local governments may top them up using local funds. Table 6.2 shows the case of Switzerland. It indicates by canton the maximum amount of additional support available as a percentage of federal unemployment benefits. The role of local benefits seems significant, but the table may overstate its message: there is in fact little local variation in rates, and these schemes usually include specific eligibility conditions.

6.3   Time Inconsistency

International agreements are considerably more fragile than contracts amongst private parties because of obvious enforcement limitations. An insurance company does not typically renege on commitments, nor do insured agents leave when unusually large compensations paid out to others result in higher premiums. A Community insurance system must face the possibility that a country – or worse, a group of countries – may be subject to a particularly bad and long-lasting shock, possibly a permanent one. If the costs are high, the incentive to renege may be overwhelming. Not only would the insurance system collapse but its demise could very well generate deep misgivings about other areas of common interest.

The solution is either to adopt an opting-out clause, to allow for the renegotiation of existing arrangements in the event of particularly large shocks, or not to get into such arrangements in the first place. Neither of the first two possibilities should be made too easy: any *ex post* change in arrangements reduces the *ex ante* value of the insurance. Can any reliance be placed on anything beyond the insurance of minor contingencies? One useful strategy is 'bunching': making insurance part and parcel of a wider agreement including other, strongly-desired Community-level arrangements (e.g. free trade, a single market), thereby using lots of little threads to weave a rather effective straitjacket.

This indeed seems the way federations address the problem. Bunching is also found within a nation: time-inconsistent behaviour is made difficult either through explicit constitutional provision through all the other bonds that make a nation. Yet, nations can dissolve, and there exist many examples of break-up for precisely these considerations: Czechoslovakia, Pakistan–Bangladesh, Malaysia–Singapore and the West Indies are recent examples of peaceful partitions. Tensions in Belgium and Italy are undoubtedly phenomena reflecting time-inconsistency temptations.

Another near-example of time inconsistency is provided by the case of German unification if a Community insurance system had existed in 1989. Some of the costs of German unification would have had to be shared among all EC members. These costs are high: estimated at DM 190 billion for 1993, they represent 6% of German GDP and 1.7% of total EC GDP; and undoubtedly they would have been higher if EC-financed because of the moral hazard aspects described above. It is not obvious that the other EC members would have shouldered these costs; none has volunteered to do so.

A denial of promised support is imaginable under truly exceptional circumstances, such as German unification. The outcome of retaliation following reneging could be devastating. At best, Germany could cut its own contributions to the Community budget; at worst it could retaliate in any of many areas of European affairs where it plays a critical role.

The time-inconsistency problem can also arise with borrowing, as when sovereign debtors unilaterally suspend debt service and then manage to extract concessions from their sovereign or private creditors. While EC countries do not currently have large external debts, a severe protracted disturbance could provide the incentive to run up debt in the expectation that it will be fully repaid. Nevertheless, capital markets have a recurring self-interest in preserving a reputation as unforgiving creditors. On balance, we consider that the borrowing approach to dealing with permanent shocks will be substantially time consistent. If this perception is shared by potential borrowers, countries experiencing permanent shocks will not be able to make much of the capital markets and, quite properly, they will begin their adjustment to the new state of affairs.

In contrast, federal fiscal stabilization acts as an *ex ante* mutual insurance fund. Its credibility is always under threat from permanent shocks, and any possibility of renegotiation not merely dilutes the value of any insurance offered *ex ante* but also opens up almost irresistible temptations for self-serving lobbying by individual countries. In such circumstances, the advantages of this approach should probably be described as fragile.

6.4 Adverse Selection

Countries deciding to insure one another had better choose their partners carefully. Even if a scheme can be designed that ignores the initial disparities in economies, countries can be perceived as good or bad risks in the future quite independently of their initial situations. (Initial disparities inherited from the past are properly dealt with through distributional or regional policies.) What makes a country a good or a bad risk is clear: its ability to deal promptly with disturbances and its perceived tendency to misbehave (provoking crises to attract transfers, reneging on commitments). The risk is that a country will always wish to link up with countries that are better risks than itself and will try to keep out those which appear less reliable. In the aggregate this is impossible.

The result can be highly undesirable. Even if all countries stand to benefit from a Community insurance programme, none may be willing to join. Alternatively, the only countries able to unite may be those perceived as the riskier ones; or else two rival groupings may emerge, the safe and the dangerous, with unpleasant, potentially disruptive, two-speed overtones.

Can the insurance system be designed in a way that makes it appealing to all member countries? It is certainly easier to sustain an existing insurance scheme than to establish a new one. Effort should thus be directed towards creating the proper incentives at inception. One solution is to make the scheme compulsory. This is how existing federations typically solve the adverse selection problem. In practice, veto power is likely to block the project if universality is a precondition for any move to fiscal federalism.

Another solution is to attract reluctant countries, in principle the better-risk ones, by offering them lower contributions to the scheme or to the whole EC budget. Yet this opens up more difficulties than it closes down. In particular, like treatment of different countries is one of the powerful weapons that the centre possesses in trying to stave off special pleading by individual member states. We should not abandon that principle lightly.

A variant on the above solution might again be to employ 'bunching' instead of differential contributions: to attract reluctant countries, concessions in other fields would be offered. While time-honoured in European affairs, such a strategy has many drawbacks. It does not solve the serious moral hazard problem, whereby each country has an incentive to pretend to dislike the insurance system in order to obtain concessions elsewhere, and it is less transparent than the differential contribution approach. Transparency is one of the other defences of the centre against pleading by the periphery; for reasons given above, we do not favour deliberately giving up transparency.

Hence, the adverse selection aspect of setting up an insurance programme is a serious problem without easy solution.

6.5 Insuring Nations

Insurance is based on pooling imperfectly correlated risks over a large number of people. Are nation states appropriate units to form component parts of a mutual insurance policy? Macroeconomic risk among a dozen or more countries is very different. Business cycles typically occur every 5–7 years. Permanent shocks like oil shocks or deep restructuring occur, say, once per generation. If they were to occur independently in member countries, risk diversification might not pose a major problem.

In fact, because of economic integration, macroeconomic shocks are not independently distributed. Figure 6.1 displays the growth rates of a number of EC countries. The degree of correlation between any pair of countries is high, typically between 0.6 and 0.7, and it is likely to increase further. Monetary union would also eliminate both a source of national divergence and the ability to insulate oneself by an appropriate change in the exchange rate. The scope for mutual insurance will be reduced (Mélitz and Vori, 1992).

The fact that cycles become increasingly synchronized implies, however, that some degree of co-insurance is automatically provided through trade. A country in recession reduces imports, thereby passing some of the recession on to its partners. In short, deepening integration makes insurance less attractive but also less necessary.

It is sometimes argued that further integration and synchronization may increase the appeal of collective borrowing. The EC could borrow abroad on behalf of its members, possibly obtaining better market conditions than individual countries. This benefit, likely to be small, must be balanced against the moral hazard problem, which is likely to be large. Countries with above-average credit ratings will not wish to participate in Community borrowing. The EC would therefore be borrowing only on behalf of its most risky member states, lowering the quality rating of the EC in capital markets.

6.6 Spillovers

Close economic integration tends to lead to cross-country spillovers that alter the incentives affecting national fiscal policies. The presence of such spillovers raises the possibility that some kind of concerted action, through either coordination or centralization, may be more efficient. Before asking whether the costs of concerted action outweigh the benefits, we first examine the benefits in more detail. Through what channels do these spillovers occur? And how might they be reduced?

Figure 6.1: GDP Growth Rates. 1956–92. Per cent.

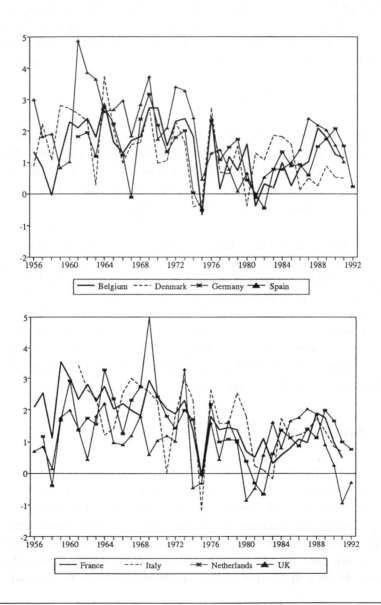

Source: IMF.

A first effect may result in insufficient fiscal stabilization. When, for example, a country undertakes expansionary fiscal measures, part of the stimulus leaks out in the form of imports from its partners who may themselves be facing similar difficulties and therefore welcome this expansion. An individual country fails to take account of the benefit conferred on its partners; it sees only the import leakage that reduces for itself the benefits of its own fiscal expansion. Since fiscal expansion does not come free – it gives rise to additional government debt that must be repaid eventually by taxpayers from within that country – each country uses fiscal expansion too little and too infrequently. The obvious solution to this particular problem is to organize fiscal policy at EC level, thereby internalizing to the decision-making process the cross-country spillovers that individual member states neglect.

A bond-financed fiscal expansion tends to raise interest rates within the national financial market. In a monetary union, with a single financial market, one country's fiscal action will affect others' costs of borrowing. In principle, this leads to an over-expansion of uncoordinated national fiscal policies: each country neglects the fact that it inflicts on its partners part of the cost of its own policy. Since this second effect pulls in the opposite direction from the first, empirical quantification is needed to make a judgement about the overall effect. Ambiguity is not the best basis for embarking on a search for a concerted solution across member states.

If the direction and magnitude of the concerted action required could be established, how should it be undertaken? A theme of earlier sections has been 'decentralize where possible, coordinate where necessary, centralize only when coordination is necessary but not credible'. Coordination would mean that countries subject their policies to each others' scrutiny and agree to take into account collective needs; but this strains credulity. The record on fiscal policy coordination for macroeconomic purposes is not encouraging. Establishing clearly agreed criteria against which to judge the need for stimulus or contraction in particular countries would be difficult. Given the uncertainty about, for example, equilibrium rates of unemployment, the temptation for strategic misrepresentation would be substantial. A second reason why the

Table 6.3: Trade Links Within Western Germany and Within EC. 1990. Percentage of GDP.

Intra-German		*Intra-EC*	
Baden-Wurttemberg	11.7	Belgium	4.0
Bavaria	7.6	Denmark	13.8
Berlin	19.0	Germany	13.8
Bremen	52.6	Greece	13.4
Hamburg	45.6	Spain	8.9
Hesse	18.7	France	12.5
Lower Saxony	18.3	Ireland	37.6
North Rhine-Westphalia	8.1	Italy	9.3
Rhineland Palatinate	20.0	Netherlands	32.7
Saarland	13.9	Portugal	24.3
Schleswig-Holstein	17.0	UK	11.6

Note: Trade links defined as the average of exports and imports as percentage of GDP.
Sources: Regional Database, *Eurostat.*

credibility of the coordination approach would be likely to be minimal is that it relies on a framework in which national Parliaments would retain ultimate responsibility for such fiscal judgements. That a national Parliament at a point in time would ever sacrifice the nation's fiscal interest for some wider good within the EC seems insufficiently probable, whatever the ease with which it could be demonstrated to be in the nation's interest on average.

To be efficient and credible, the basis for *ex post* coordination would have to be decided *ex ante*. In this instance, a transfer of some fiscal power to the centre seems the only realistic possibility if the collective best is to be pursued; that, indeed, is how existing federations solve problem. For example, trade links among German Länder are not markedly tighter than among EC countries, as shown in Table 6.3. The smaller Länder are of course very open, but so too are small countries Spillovers are therefore of the same relative magnitude. Yet, the Länder run much smaller budget imbalances than countries. For example in 1992, a year when the German economy started to slow down, the deficits of Länder governments amounted to 1% of GDP while the federal budget deficit stood at 3.2%.

6.7   Limitations Imposed by the Maastricht Treaty

So far we have assumed that each government can borrow subject only to its long-run budget constraint. Under the provisions of the Maastricht Treaty, this will not be the case: the Treaty imposes ceilings on the size of government deficits and public debts. Most countries are now well above the 60% public debt limit and may have to forgo active fiscal policy for years, even decades, to come. This may just be a transitory limitation; eventually, all member countries may fall below the debt threshold, providing scope for temporary fiscal expansion when needed. However, the 3% budget deficit constraint will never wash away; nor is it a moderate constraint. Figure 6.2 shows that, for most countries, the limit would often have been binding during the last two decades.

One approach is to apply the constraint more flexibly. Even the Treaty admits exceptions and calls for a careful process of mutual surveillance. What would have happened in 1993 if Europe had already been operating under this clause? The average deficit was nearly 6% of GDP, but significant parts of these deficits are cyclical. Even though in 1993 Maastricht remained a long way off, most countries refrained from fiscal expansion.

Thus, it is safe to conclude that the budget constraint will play an active role, if only by inducing self-restraint. With national policies thus emasculated, the pressure for centralized action may become unavoidable, as is the case in most federations. Local governments often face statutory limits, as noted above. Central government, free of any such constraint, will be led to undertake active fiscal policy stabilization.

The Maastricht Treaty is internally inconsistent. It calls for subsidiarity which would discourage the emergence of active EC-level fiscal

Figure 6.2: Government Deficits and Maastricht Ceiling.
1960–93. Per cent of GDP.

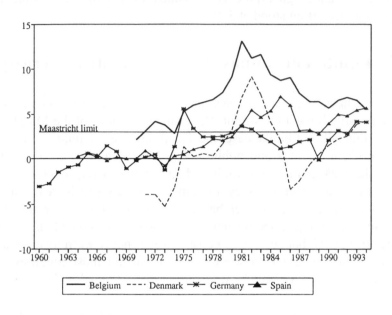

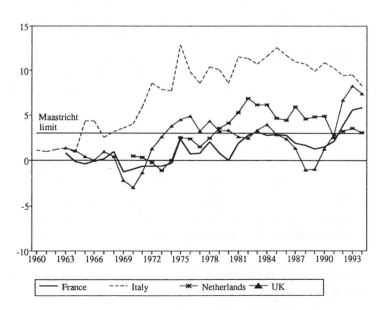

stabilization; yet, by establishing very tough 'prudential rules', it will act as a powerful incentive to break the subsidiarity principle. As a corollary, if fiscal policy should remain at the national level, the Maastricht Treaty's provisions must be either suppressed or implemented with considerable flexibility.

Not only will this contradiction plague the long run, when the monetary union is in place; it will also render the transition to EMU perilous, to the point of threatening the ultimate goal itself. The exchange crises of 1992–3 have made it abundantly clear that markets are alarmed by the absence of policies in the face of a recession: not only has coordination been conspicuously absent, but national authorities have also displayed surprising reluctance to use fiscal policies. The costs of the Maastricht inconsistency have already been enormous.

6.8 Conclusion

On balance, we cannot make a convincing case for centralizing fiscal policy for macroeconomic stabilization. Even though EC-level insurance is appealing, too many drawbacks undermine that case. Insurance is unappealing because it generates perverse behaviour and attracts only the higher-risk countries. Usual solutions adopted by existing federations imply compulsory membership and harmonization of relevant institutions. Thus, centralization inevitably spreads.

Some limited degree of Community-level stabilization could be possible if proper action were taken to limit the defects of centralized insurance. Moral hazard could be mitigated by schemes that penalize perverse behaviour. For example, only a relatively small part of macroeconomic shocks could be covered by the Community-level insurance scheme. Individual countries would be left to cope with the rest, through borrowing, which might be needed if only to address the problem created by the Maastricht Treaty's limitation on budget deficits.

This appears to leave the Community with a stark dilemma. The Maastricht limit on borrowing threatens to set up pressures to centralize fiscal policy because national policy is no longer adequate to the task, as we saw from the pervasive failure to use fiscal policy to cope with the recession of 1992–3. Embarking on fiscal centralization is likely to unleash Leviathan pressures and weaken accountability. Yet the Maastricht limits on fiscal policy were the explicit policy response, albeit in our judgement not the most appropriate one, to fear of a different aspect of government failure, namely the inability of many national governments to resist short-run temptations to bloat budgets and print money. A commitment to permanently fixed exchange rates prevents individual countries from using exchange rate changes to insulate themselves from macroeconomic misbehaviour elsewhere in the EC.

Forced to choose between these competing dangers, in this case we have little hesitation. If or when monetary union is attained, an independent central bank provides the appropriate commitment to price stability; knowing that they are unable to print money to finance deficits, member states will then have to pursue more responsible fiscal policies.

7　Subsidiarity and Regulatory Policy

In this chapter we provide brief illustrations of the principles developed in Chapter 3 in a number of areas of regulation of the economy. As will be seen, our conclusions are strikingly different across different areas of policy.

7.1　Competition Policy: Mergers, Takeovers and Joint Ventures

Competition policy provides a particularly interesting illustration of the arguments developed in Chapter 3, for two reasons. First, in the specific area of merger policy the European Community has undertaken its most explicit attempt to allocate power of jurisdiction between the Community's institutions and those of member states, in accordance with the principles underlying the subsidiarity doctrine. The Merger Regulation, which came into force in 1990, stipulates that mergers, acquisitions or what are known as 'concentrative' joint ventures between parties whose combined aggregate world-wide annual turnover exceeds 5 billion ECU should be notified to the European Commission, *unless the parties conduct two-thirds or more of their business in one and the same member state.* This rider is a clear and precise attempt to base centralization upon the extent of the spillovers between member states, since it exempts from EC jurisdiction cases where the effects of the merger are primarily concentrated within one member state.

The second reason why merger policy is interesting is that we have more detailed evidence on the nature of accountability and its failures than is available in most other areas of regulatory policy. Our arguments in Chapter 3 imply that the case for centralizing merger policy involves trading off the gains from internalizing spillovers against any costs in increased regulatory capture. In a study of the first two-and-a-half years of operation of the Regulation, Neven, Nuttall and Seabright (1993) addressed the question of the extent to which centralization may be expected to change the character of regulatory capture. Their chief findings were that the procedure implemented by the Commission, while impressively speedy and efficient in an administrative sense, is unnecessarily systematic and also lacks transparency. This may be expected, they suggest, to give well-informed firms significant bargaining power in their dealings with the Commission, and consequently to distort the policy in the direction of a greater tolerance of market power than is either desirable or consistent with the apparent aims of the Regulation.

Such a claim receives some support from a survey of firms involved in merger cases before the Commission. This indicated a high level of satisfaction with the procedure, which was particularly marked among German firms, whose alternative would have been an investigation by the Bundeskartellamt (the German Federal Cartel Office). It also highlighted the various means used by companies to mobilize lobbying pressures in support of their case and the limited opportunities available to other interested parties (such as consumers) to do the same. The authors do not conclude, however, that centralization is after all a mistake. They suggest rather that the risk of regulatory capture at the centre, which might otherwise offset the benefits of centralization, can be contained by reforms to increase the transparency of the system and strengthen the influence of those interests (such as consumers) that stand to lose from the exercise of market power.

This area of policy illustrates a number of points of importance in our discussion in Chapter 3. First, the gains from coordination of policy between member states are related to the magnitude of the spillovers involved; where these are related to variables that can be approximately measured (such as business turnover), jurisdiction can be allocated on a case-by-case basis rather than entirely to one level of government. (Nevertheless, see Neven *et al*, pp. 196–201, for a discussion of the two-thirds rule and alternative ways of measuring spillovers.)

Second, merger control is an area in which cooperation to secure the benefits of policy coordination is a particularly unsatisfactory alternative to centralization, because of the highly discretionary nature of the policy to be implemented and the consequent difficulty for twelve member states in observing whether each is abiding by the terms of a collective agreement. It is interesting to contrast the centralization of power in the European Community with the procedure for cooperation between the competition authorities of the EC and the EFTA states initiated by the Agreement establishing the European Economic Area (see Stragier, 1993). It is likely that two entities can trust each other better than twelve to take their mutual interests into account when implementing competition policy.

Third, the gains from centralization and the costs from diminished accountability can here be evaluated in similar terms. Centralization enables the approval of efficiency-enhancing mergers that would otherwise be prevented (and the prevention of market-power-increasing mergers that would otherwise be approved) because of insufficient attention to the gains and costs to shareholders, workers and consumers who happen to be located outside the borders of the member state with jurisdiction in the given case. Centralization may also encourage the approval of undesirable or desirable mergers because of distortions in the relative lobbying power of the various interest groups, which may change in importance according to the level of jurisdiction involved.

Fourth, if Neven *et al*'s analysis is accurate, merger control is an instance in which 'government failure' does not necessarily lead to Leviathan – that is, to excessive levels of taxing and spending (or excessively tight regulation). On the contrary, the disproportion in the lobbying power of firms and consumers may in some circumstances lead to excessively lax regulation. Competition between jurisdictions may then actually worsen the government failure (since firms and their acquisition strategies are much more mobile than consumers among countries).

Overall, merger policy is a good illustration of a case where the gains from centralization are high; but it is also a warning that the central institutions need to be designed in such a way as to ensure these gains are not dissipated through an increase in rent-seeking and regulatory capture.

7.2 Environmental Regulation

Since the Single European Act, environmental issues have been given official standing as a matter for European policy, cited in the same breath as agriculture. How subsidiarity should apply to this field is not always clear in Community documents: the Commission's report, 'European Community Programme of Policy and Action in Relation to the Environment and Sustainable Development' (C 138/5), in effect interprets the principle of subsidiarity as leaving to the member states the implementation of policies decided at the European level. The Council, in resolution 93/C 138/01 in which it accepts the general orientation of this report, stresses the fact that concrete policy proposals must be consistent with the principle of subsidiarity, and it indicates that the Council will ensure that such proposals meet this standard. All this opens up two important questions: How much European intervention in environmental policy does the subsidiarity policy allow? And which products and which activities can be regulated on the basis of this principle?

Economic theory sees an environmental problem when an agent's activity damages the natural resources available to another agent. The proper jurisdiction depends on the extent of the externality created. Loud music played in a house isolated in the countryside falls under the jurisdiction of the family that suffers from their teenager's taste. Played in an apartment building, it falls under the jurisdiction of the management. Played in the street or through open windows, it falls under the jurisdiction of the municipality. Finally, supersonic booms may require national or international restraints.

In the case of pollution, on which we shall focus our attention, it is convenient to distinguish three types of environmental activities: first, those whose effects are restricted to the territory of individual countries, such as that affecting drinking water provided to households; second, those located in one country of the Community which affect others; third, those that affect the world in its entirety, such as the burning of fossil fuels or the emission of chlorofluorocarbon (CFC) gases. The arguments for European involvement in these three cases are substantially different.

7.2.1 Drinking Water

The Council Directive (80/778/EC) of 15 July 1980 regulates the 'quality of water intended for human consumption'. It sets minimal quality standards defined in terms of colour, odour and taste, and it limits the concentration of a number of substances (hydrogen ions, sodium, potassium and so on). The quality of the water drunk by a Dane does not change the welfare of a Spaniard, and there is *prima-facie* evidence that this directive flies in the face of the principle of subsidiarity. National governments should be responsible for activities that affect only the welfare of their citizens. (By the same token, within each country, according to the theory of fiscal federalism, the regulation of water quality should be decentralized to local governments.)

How can the Council defend its decision to take this role? 'Whereas a disparity between provisions already applicable or in the process of being drawn up in the various Member States relating to the quality of water for human consumption may create differences in the conditions of competition and, as a result, directly affect the operation of the common market. . . ' To put it more simply, the Council seeks to prevent 'ecological dumping'. It is concerned that member states may try to give their own firms a competitive advantage by lowering the environmental standards that they impose, and that this non-cooperative behaviour will result in a general under-protection of the environment. But could this really apply to drinking water?

Our discussion of fiscal competition in Chapter 4 emphasized that quantitative environmental standards, as a form of implicit taxation, may be subject to the kinds of distortion fiscal competition can cause. This may be a theoretical possibility, but how can we decide whether it is a serious risk in practice? It is sometimes argued that ecological dumping can be diagnosed if environmental standards differ across countries.[1] But this is neither a *sufficient* condition (the costs as well as the benefits of environmental protection can vary widely between countries, so there is no reason to expect common standards to be optimal) nor even a *necessary* condition (two countries might have the same standards but set these inefficiently low because each fears competition from the other).

Why might they do this? In particular, what reason could countries have to use low environmental standards to attract mobile capital, rather than (say) subsidies or low tax rates? For one thing, explicit subsidies may be illegal (and they do indeed violate the Community's rules against state aids). On the other hand, our discussion in Chapter 4 suggested that undesirable fiscal competition is most likely to result from instruments that can be targeted on marginally mobile factors. While this may be true of some environmental standards (smoke emissions or land-use restrictions, which can be modified for some firms without creating precedents for large numbers of others), drinking water standards are at the opposite end of the spectrum. It is impossible to relax drinking water standards for marginally mobile factors without relaxing them (and incurring a corresponding social cost) for all polluting factors, whether potentially mobile or not. Any government wishing to attract mobile factors of production would be insane to do so by allowing its drinking water to be polluted. If countries choose different drinking water standards, it is only reasonable to suppose that these are the standards they (or their governments) prefer.

There may, of course, be independent reasons for thinking that the political process in some countries already results in inefficient levels of pollution, a situation that competition between countries may exacerbate. For instance, countries that regulate the environment by setting Pigovian taxes are in principle in a position to compare the costs of environmental pollution with its benefits in an optimal manner. If they regulate by setting quantitative standards, however, the benefits of pollution are kept by firms instead of being distributed to taxpayers. Since, with integrated capital markets, some of the owners of firms are foreigners, inadequate consideration may be given to the benefits of pollution; but in this case the result of competition between jurisdictions would be that standards would be too tight rather than too lax.

To summarize, then, it is certainly possible in theory for environmental regulation to be too lax as a result of competition to attract mobile capital. This risk is particularly serious if lax regulation is easier to keep hidden than direct subsidies (which may be illegal). Thus, there is a case for coordinating some environmental regulation at the EC level to avoid the inefficiencies resulting from competition to attract mobile tax bases. This argument does not, however, provide a blanket justification for EC intervention. In particular, drinking water standards are most unlikely to be the means by which this competition takes place since they are hard to target on mobile factors. The presence of other distortions is as likely to make regulation too tight as too lax. There is no case, then, for centralizing the regulation of drinking water standards, and the Council's efforts in this regard are inconsistent with the principle of susidiarity. It is quite possible, of course, that the Council's chosen standards in a particular instance may be 'better' in some sense than those of member states. But there is no *systematic* reason to think the EC is more likely to get the balance right than member states, and subsidiarity accordingly recommends that the latter should decide.

This does not mean that the EC should be inactive in this field. Knowledge and understanding of environmental phenomena is very incomplete, and they necessitate the study of complex systems whose behaviour is hard to predict. Even when there is no direct externality due to pollution, there exist externalities in the production of scientific knowledge. It is an entirely appropriate responsibility for European institutions to promote the creation and dissemination of this knowledge. In this respect, the design of new standards of measurement and reporting of the quality of the environment and their standardization can play a useful role. (Directive 77/795/EEC on the Exchange of Information about Surface Fresh Water or the Directive 79/869/EEC on Drinking Water Measurement are two good examples.)

7.2.2 Pollution of the Rhine

We now want to apply the principle of subsidiarity to cross-border pollution, using the example of the River Rhine. Fifty million people, in Austria, Belgium, France, Germany, Liechtenstein, Luxembourg, the

Netherlands and Switzerland, live in its watershed. The industrial boom in Germany, Switzerland and the Netherlands after the Second World War (in 1992 20% of the world chemical industry was estimated to be located in the Rhine basin) is widely acknowledged as having accelerated a deterioration that began in the nineteenth century. The pollution reached its peak in the 1970s when the Rhine was called the 'most romantic sewer in Europe'. Between 1975 and 1985, considerable efforts were made to clean the river. Pollution with organic substances consuming oxygen fell by about 50%, while pollution from cadmium fell by about 90%. On 1 November 1986, however, a fire spread through a chemical warehouse owned by the firm Sandoz, in Basel, Switzerland, which caused disastrous damage to the ecosystem. This event showed that the river was not sufficiently protected and provoked a public outcry. As a consequence, the environment ministers of the countries belonging to the International Commission for the Protection of the Rhine (ICPR) – France, Germany, Luxembourg, the Netherlands and Switzerland, and the EC – agreed a Rhine Action Plan (RAP) with three main goals. First, higher species and especially salmon should again become indigenous; second, the river should be fit for production of drinking water; third, sediment toxicity should be reduced to a point where it could safely be used for landfill or dumped in the sea. To these targets, a fourth was added in 1989: to improve the water quality of the North Sea, there should be major reductions in the amounts of nitrogen and phosphorus entering it from the Rhine.

Although much remains to be done, progress has been spectacular. In 1990, 120 invertebrate species could be found in the river, whereas in 1970 that figure was 27. Dick Hogervorst, head of the permanent technical-scientific secretariat of the ICPR, is quoted as saying that the water quality is high enough for salmon to return.[2]

It is impossible to review the Rhine programme in its entirety, but a number of features with general applicability are worth examining in more detail. First, the choice of both targets and mechanisms has been rather little informed by economic analysis. The RAP demands that each industry use the 'best available technical means', aiming at a reduction of pollution of at least 50% between 1985 and 1995. The costs and benefits of reducing pollution from different sources do not appear to have been calculated, and the choice of the sectors to be targeted does not seem to be based upon well-defined criteria. Industrial pollution has been reduced substantially, but pollution from agriculture and towns is still high. The marginal costs of reducing pollution from different sources have not been equalized. This may partly be due to the fact that industrial pollution can be traced to its source, and the party that causes it enjoined to stop. In the case of agriculture and towns (for which rain water is a main agent of pollution), it is much more difficult convincingly to pinpoint the damage caused by a single agent. Solutions do exist, though: reduction in the use of fertilizers and pesticides, and the purification of rain water in urban areas.

The choice of the return of salmon as the first objective of the RAP also deserves comment. The annual salmon catch had fallen from a high of 250,000 in 1885 to zero after 1940. Even if we put the value of a salmon at an exorbitant 50 ECUs, the value of the catch is dwarfed by, for instance, the DM 1,362 million spent by BASF alone in 1991 on new and existing environmental measures. Even if we include the value of all other fish that can be caught in the river, the figures do not add up. It may well be that the aesthetic value of a clean river warrants the size of the investments that are made: people who have never seen the Rhine might find utility in the knowledge that it is clean. On the other hand, it seems remarkable that the programme has made no systematic quantified estimates of the benefits of a reduction in pollution, notwithstanding the necessary arbitrariness and imprecision of these types of estimate.

The third striking feature of the Rhine agreements has been the need to renegotiate them. The case of salt from the French potassium mines provides a striking example. This salt pollutes the Rhine, and the Dutch who must fight continuously against salt infiltration from the sea have for years put pressure on the French government to stop this source of pollution. The Bonn Convention, signed before the Sandoz fire, required France to reduce the amount of salt dumped in the Rhine from 110 to 70 kilograms per second. Given that salt is an unavoidable by-product of the production of potassium, substantial sums had to be set aside for its storage. At the ninth conference of the environment ministers of the countries bordering the Rhine, the Dutch minister announced that her country would not participate in the application of the second part of the accord. She argued that the share of the expenses borne by the Netherlands would be more usefully employed in the reduction of other pollutants such as phosphates and chemical products. The example yields an important lesson: agreements to reduce pollution need to be flexible enough to take into account new information. They should be written in such a way as to facilitate appropriate renegotiations, although this may sometimes imply deviations from the 'polluter pays' principle. If under the original agreement, France had borne all the costs of salt removal, the relaxation of standards when new information became available would have been more difficult, as the Netherlands would have had no incentive to accept it.[3]

Forgetting for a moment that the RAP involves a non-EC country, what are the lessons that can be drawn in terms of subsidiarity? There are clearly spillovers – literally – between the countries involved. But is there a case for managing these joint environmental resources directly from Brussels instead of by agreement among nation states as at present? Certainly, a well-designed independent European agency for the environment would provide more flexibility in environmental management. The need to take into account the difficulties of renegotiation when drawing up agreements would be substantially reduced: the agency could unilaterally, or with the approval of the other relevant European institutions, adapt regulations to new information. This flexibility may of course have costs, as we discussed in Section 3.5: it might make countries less willing to cooperate with the programme in the first place (fearing that its future actions might be harder to control). This is probably not a serious concern in the case of the Rhine, however, where the perceived benefits from coordinated policies seem to be high.

Does the fact that cooperation has appeared to work well so far mean that there is no case for centralization? Not necessarily. We have already suggested that the costs of the reductions achieved may have been inefficiently high: could these represent in part the costs of a cooperative rather than a centralized agreement? Three reasons suggest themselves. First, the need to monitor the cooperation of each country may have biased the policy towards easily observed targets (the return of salmon, the 'best available technical means' and so on) and away from others that make better economic sense. Much depends on whether an EC environment agency would be able in its turn to overcome pressures for visible 'results' that would have the same effect. Second, the bias towards reducing industrial pollution and away from limits on agricultural and urban pollution may be likewise due to the fact that countries' cooperation is easier to monitor in the industrial sector. Third (and related), the temptation for countries to free-ride in agriculture is particularly great given that they participate in the benefits of this pollution in the form of increased transfers from other EC funds. A European agency would be less prone to these types of distortion.[4] On the other hand the pressures for capture of a European agency might be very great and have hardly been given systematic attention. Our above remarks about drinking water suggest such an agency might be pressurized into inappropriate degrees of uniformity in developing a policy for the EC as a whole. In sum, there is a case for centralization, but it would yield net benefits only if the agency concerned were sensitive to the need for regional diversity and decentralized implementation of its overall policy, which there is no reason to take for granted.[5]

7.2.3 European Participation in Global Environmental Regulation

A third area of environmental intervention consists in participation in international conferences on the environment, and in the negotiation of international treaties to reduce global warming or the threat to the ozone layer. Here it is clear that the potential benefits from coordinated policies are vast, and also that centralized intervention on a global scale is not an option. But we can still ask whether there is a case for EC countries to participate in such negotiations as a group rather than individually. Although hypotheses about the outcomes of large multi-party negotiations are necessarily tentative, two consequences might be expected from such collective participation. First, small countries are more likely to be able to get away with free-riding behaviour in which they let other countries carry the burden of the reduction of pollution while taking advantage of its benefit. Hence, merging environmental policies among EC countries will probably increase the share of the effort borne by Europe. Second, large countries are more credible when threatening sanctions against countries that do not abide by the terms of global agreements. Hence merging environmental policies among EC countries will probably increase the efficiency of world-wide cooperative efforts to improve the environment.

7.3   Agriculture

In contrast with our discussion of competition policy in Section 7.1, agriculture provides a striking example of some of the costs of inappropriate centralization of the power to regulate markets. Spillovers between countries in agriculture are not particularly great, and the nature of the policies implemented (price support funded by a common budget so that its costs are shared between countries in proportions unrelated to the benefits they perceive) has created wide disparities in the net impact of the Common Agricultural Policy (CAP) on member countries. Net beneficiaries of the CAP have a powerful incentive – and the *de facto* veto has until recently given them the ability – to resist reform. Paradoxically, therefore, a sector in which spillovers were initially small has through centralization created large artificial spillovers whose presence has seriously distorted negotiations on the future of regulation.

Agricultural markets are potentially among the most competitive markets in any economy. Spillovers between countries are small, but they are not negligible, for two reasons. First, differences between countries and regions in climate and natural resource endowments lead to specialization; producers in some countries therefore have a degree of collective market power that they do not enjoy individually. On standard optimum tariff arguments this may create a case for centralized power to raise prices above collective levels in order to exploit their market power, and it is the exercise of this power that results in international spillovers. (The result is inefficient for the world as a whole but may be in the interests of individual countries.) Second, and more important, labour employed in agriculture is probably harder to redeploy quickly in other activities than that in any other sector. (Populations move out of agriculture as generations retire, but individuals are much less mobile.) Another way to express this is by saying that mobility costs create a rent to labour in agriculture, a rent that is threatened by imports and by competition in world markets.

Concern about spillovers of this second kind was a strong factor in leading to the inclusion of agriculture in the Treaty of Rome, and to the establishment of a Common Agricultural Policy, which after a transitional period established in 1967 the system of common support prices that has in essence persisted until today. France in particular felt that the ability of its agricultural sector to penetrate German markets would be threatened by a system of national policies, which would lead to restrictions on agricultural trade and a downward bidding of support prices to inefficiently low levels.

In fact, it is now widely appreciated that assistance to the agricultural sector through the price support scheme has been a disaster and that any downward pressure on support prices could only have been welcome. The policy has resulted in over-production and surpluses that have to be stored or disposed of at great cost; it has not primarily helped poorer farmers since the benefits of price support have accrued mainly to the owners of land (the scarce factor) and to large farms; it has resulted in over-capitalization and excessive fertilizer and pesticide use, thus exacerbating pollution. The policy has raised food prices to consumers, a highly regressive form of implicit taxation; and it has not even contributed greatly towards self-sufficiency (an original aim), since reduced imports of agricultural products have been offset by increased dependence on imported inputs, especially energy (Winters, 1991). Agricultural support takes up nearly 60% of the Community's budget, and its cost rose twenty-five times from 1968 to 1989.[6] Table 7.1 shows the evolution in real terms since 1980 of expenditure from the price support fund (EAGGF), from which it can be seen that it rose by over 40% when GNP rose by just over 20%. It was also becoming progressively more expensive per unit of agricultural output, which rose by less than 14% over the same period. And it did not prevent employment in agriculture from falling by 25%.

Table 7.1: Indices of Real Agricultural Expenditure, GNP, Output and Employment. 1980–9 (1980 = 100).

	Real Agricultural Expenditure (EAGGF)	EC Real GNP	Agricultural Output	Agricultural Employment
1981	89.0	100.1	99.1	95.0
1982	91.7	101.0	104.5	91.8
1983	110.4	102.7	104.9	89.5
1984	121.0	105.1	108.0	87.3
1985	125.5	107.6	107.9	85.9
1986	136.9	110.5	110.1	83.2
1987	138.4	113.8	110.0	80.9
1988	160.6	118.3	112.1	75.3
1989	142.5	122.2	113.3	75.0

Source: *Green Europe*, 1992, no. 1.

Though many individual countries implement expensive and inefficient schemes of agricultural price support, it seems likely that centralization exacerbated the EC's problems. First, as many authors have emphasized, the net benefits and costs of the policy are very unequally distributed (see Winters, 1987, Table 2), since the predominantly agricultural countries (such as France and Italy) are net beneficiaries while the policy has large aggregate costs (see for example Buckwell *et al*, 1982; OECD, 1990). The Luxembourg compromise in 1966 effectively gave these beneficiaries the ability to prevent reform, and for other countries to buy them off by offering direct transfers would have risked exposing the high costs of the policy to Europe's taxpayers and consumers of food, of which many were (and still are) unaware.

We emphasized in Section 3.5 that unanimity voting requirements tend to entrench the status quo. Until 1984 the status quo for European agriculture was unambiguous: it was the existing price support rules. Once the budgetary costs resulting from these rules threatened to breach the ceiling on national VAT contributions to the Community budget, however, as they did in that year, the status quo (defined in budgetary terms) became incompatible with the rules of price support. This changed the balance of negotiating power in favour of the net contributing countries (such as the UK). The reforms of the CAP since 1986 can largely be attributed to this shift. The extent to which they outweigh the previous effects of centralization in exacerbating the pressure towards inefficient policies is uncertain, but the overall lesson is very clear: centralizing policy on the basis of perceived spillovers, without attention to the distortionary incentives established by the central procedure adopted, can be a very grave mistake. Unless the spillovers are very large and cannot be dealt with by coordinated national policies (as would certainly be possible in agriculture), centralization should be avoided. And if there is to be a central policy, it should not be designed in such a way that powerful parties benefit from inefficient outcomes.

7.4   Regional Policy and the Structural Funds

In some respects the Common Agricultural Policy can be seen as the European Community's first attempt at regional policy. It now has an explicit budget for regional policy in the form of the so-called Structural Funds. These account for around 25% of the EC budget and nearly 0.3% of EC GDP. Is there any reason to think that the centralization of the Community's second attempt at regional policy is any better conceived than its first?

Structural Funds consist of the European Regional Development Fund (ERDF), the European Social Fund (ESF) and the Guidance component of the European Agricultural Guidance and Guarantee Fund (EAGGF). The main objectives of the ERDF are to promote development and assist structural adjustment in less developed regions and to assist areas affected by industrial decline. The means are primarily the finance of large-scale infrastructure projects and, to a lesser extent, industrial investment projects. The ESF is concerned with unemployment and labour market issues. Disbursements are largely on vocational training and are concentrated on disadvantaged regions of the EC. The much smaller structural fund element of the EAGGF is devoted to adjustment and investment in agriculture. Receipts from the ERDF and ESF amounted to 2.7% of Portuguese, 2.8% of Greek and 2.4% of Irish GDP in 1992.

The case for an EC-wide regional policy rests on several arguments. The first is equity. Differences between national and regional income levels within the EC are well documented. Although it is more natural to think of equity in terms of inter-personal than inter-regional differences, the goal of narrowing regional income differences is incorporated in the Single European Act. And concern for the political cohesion of the Community is also founded on the judgement that this is more likely to be threatened by inter-regional disparities than by equivalent disparities among individuals within the same region.

The second argument is in terms of efficiency. A neoclassical view suggests that increased goods trade should lead automatically to a diminution of regional wage differences, as regions specialize according to comparative advantage. Capital mobility should accelerate this process, as capital moves to low-wage regions. According to this view, policy is unnecessary, as the single market – combined perhaps with policy to liberalize regional or national labour market imperfections – is sufficient to move the EC towards internal 'factor price equalization'. If this convergence does not occur, then it is either due to underlying differences in endowments or to market failures to which policy should be directly targeted.

An alternative view suggests that forces for regional convergence are not automatic, and, more strikingly, that free goods trade and increased capital mobility may increase rather than reduce regional wage differences.[7] This can arise if firms are operating under increasing returns to scale. When trade barriers are relatively high, firms have to operate close to the markets they supply, so a particular industry may operate in many regions. As the cost of inter-regional or international trade is reduced, firms will exploit economies of scale by concentrating production at fewer locations. And, as long as trade costs are not zero, they will want to locate close to large markets – in 'central' as opposed to 'peripheral' regions. According to this view, market integration may encourage the concentration of economic activity. Wage differences in central regions will increase as integration is pursued, and wages in peripheral regions may decline.

These arguments are dependent on the diagnosis of some sort of market failure. This may come simply from increasing returns to scale internal to firms and imperfect competition which generate linkages (or pecuniary externalities) between firms; or it may be based on the existence of technological externalities between firms. The welfare economics of these imperfect economies are complex and it is not immediately clear whether they provide a case for regional policy. For example, if there are positive benefits from firms' agglomeration, this should not be discouraged, but it is easy to imagine situations where there is a case for policy. Movement of a firm or worker from a peripheral to a central area may make the latter worse off – for example, if there are congestion externalities. And it may also make the peripheral area worse off if remaining firms suffer from loss of linkages or demand from the moving firm or worker. This effect concerns more than one jurisdiction, and in principle it gives rise to a case for policy coordination (but not necessarily for centralization).

The balance of the efficiency arguments is far from clear. The equity argument suggests direct transfers and policy to bring about relocation of economic activity, but it is not easy to see what form such policy should take. The spillovers from different activities are difficult to identify. Infrastructure development to make outlying regions less peripheral is a possible policy, but the ambiguous effects of reducing the costs of trade have already been noted. There is considerable uncertainty whether Structural Fund expenditure to date has been effective other than merely as a form of income transfer between Europe's regions.

If, as seems plausible, some albeit imperfect methods of identifying externality-generating investments can be refined, and these create an efficiency as well as an equity case for regional policy, can we say anything about its implementation? What should be the respective roles of central and regional authority in this process?

Two polar cases can be imagined. One is the case in which the EC simply distributes funds to the lower-level jurisdiction to spend (or not) as the latter sees fit. The other is the case in which the central authority takes direct responsibility for project selection and implementation. Successive reforms of the Structural Funds have moved in the direction of centralization. Since its establishment the ERDF has allocated funds to particular projects, but these were initially within predetermined national allocations of funds. Concerns about additionality – the extent to which ERDF resources represent additional aid, or merely replace national programmes – led in the 1970s to a proportion of the ERDF being allocated outside the predetermined national quotas. The reform of 1989 moved further in this direction. Nations submit regional plans to the Commission, and the Community Support Framework for the region is then drawn up in consultations between lower-level jurisdictions and the Commission. In this way the priorities of the central authority (articulated in a series of objectives) are important in deciding the package of intervention measures to be followed.

What are the relative merits of centralized versus decentralized implementation of regional policy? First, it is important to note that neither scheme guarantees additionality. National and local government expenditure plans will – and should – be adjusted in the light of EC financing of projects.

One set of arguments turns on the economic efficiency of policy implementation. In favour of centralization is the fact that central control can enable cross-regional and cross-national comparisons of projects. Thus the likelihood that 'good' projects in one country are left unfinanced while 'less good' projects in another go ahead is reduced. Projects may also span countries – as with the integrated Mediterranean programmes – creating a case for central coordination, if not central direction. But few such projects concern more than two countries, so coordination is probably feasible without centralization. And tending against centralization are the informational concerns we have noted elsewhere in this Report. Efficient selection of projects requires detailed local knowledge. Central authorities may not have this knowledge and, critically, lower tiers have an incentive to misrepresent in order to manipulate the process of resource allocation. Although the problem may be mitigated by partnership in the construction of the Community Support Framework and by cost sharing (as in ERDF and ESF projects), it may not be eliminated. There remain strong incentives for regions to put forward projects not on grounds of economic merit but rather in order to manipulate the process of allocation of funds.

A further set of arguments relates to the possible mismatch between the preferences of the central authority and of lower-level jurisdictions. Essentially the centre may want control because it does not trust regions to spend the money appropriately. Clearly, care must be taken with this argument. We have argued elsewhere that democratic accountability is probably greater at the local and national levels than at the EC level. But the case for transfer of power to the centre can be made on two grounds; the first turns on the willingness of net contributors to participate in the scheme, and the second on political failure at the lower level.

To illustrate the first of these arguments, suppose that resources are allocated in the decentralized mode, and that each recipient region has two possible ways of spending money allocated to it, project A and project B. Both are worth while, and the local government with full information and pursuing agreed objectives of regional development – knows that A is better, and chooses it. Contributor regions are only willing to participate in the scheme, however, if a majority of recipient regions undertake project B. In this case the decentralized system may break down – donors refuse to participate. A centralized system can survive by selecting project B. This achieves the consensus that allows the scheme to operate and brings with it net benefits but these are smaller than those the decentralized system would have yielded had it been able to survive. Examples of this phenomenon are widespread – for example, the pursuit of high-profile projects by Third World aid agencies. Centralization leads to the selection of the wrong projects, but it is better than the withdrawal of contributors and collapse of the programme.

The second argument turns on political failure in the region. It is often argued that short-term pressures on regional governments cause deviation from 'optimal' policies, and that governments could do better if they could commit to policies. This argument is most frequently made in the context of control of inflation, leading to the idea of an independent central bank as a commitment device. So too with regional policy. Short-term political pressure may divert government from longer-term regional investment programmes. Central control may then provide a commitment device which is in the long-term interest of all parties – local as well as central authorities.

Both of these arguments suggest that the EC is likely to play an important role in the evaluation of development projects in its regions. This might be true even if the only motivation were equity – the desire to make transfers between regions – so long as Europe's richer countries were more willing to make such transfers when they could be reassured by the EC's participation, and its poorer countries were more able to make credible policy commitments. And to the extent that there are identifiable externalities there may be an argument on efficiency grounds as well.

But both arguments suggest that the part played by the EC in this process is essentially that of guarantor of the quality of investments undertaken with the funds transferred. It provides technical assistance to regions in the selection of projects, and it authenticates the value of these projects for the benefit of potentially sceptical net contributors. These roles clearly warrant an EC presence in the coordination of transfers among the regions within its borders, but they do not provide a convincing case for centralization as such. Centralization of the power to determine projects rests on the hypothesis that the EC systematically knows better than its regions what the best projects are (a view subsidiarity would rightly reject), or else that spillovers among regions are too complex for coordination to cope with (a view for which there is scant evidence). And centralization creates problems of its own, notably the incentive for member states to submit projects to manipulate the allocation of funds rather than because they believe these to be the most deserving of finance.

7.5 The European Satellite Industry

The European satellite communications industry is one in which externalities across countries are large. Any benefits of decentralization in terms of greater product variety are likely to be small because the products are homogeneous, and coordination between countries seems unlikely to be effective. There is therefore a strong case for allocating competence to the Community in the area of satellite communications policy.

The industry consists of two components: satellite operations and the retailing of satellite capacity to final users (TV stations, telephone and private network operators). At present, entry into the satellite operations industry is regulated at the national level and subject to coordination at the international level.

The 'slots' for satellites in space (their location both in orbit and in radio frequency) are allocated by international convention to governments. Each government in Europe can apply for slots to the International Telecommunications Union (ITU), on behalf of public or private operators. Some coordination occurs at the level of the ITU, but this organization has no real executive power.

At the same time, a satellite located over Europe can reach not only the country that owns the right to use its slot but also neighbouring countries. In practice, most satellites located over Europe have a similar reach (known as a 'footprint'), which includes all EC and EFTA countries. In Europe all slots are taken up by public telecommunications or government satellites, except for the slots of Luxembourg, which are granted by the Luxembourg government to SES/ASTRA – a private firm.

The current situation illustrates the difficulty of relying on a negotiated solution when there are strong externalities. National governments appear to bid non-cooperatively for orbits and frequencies, and this entails substantial costs. The number of slots that can be used over

Europe is limited, but all slots have *de facto* a European footprint. Governments therefore have an incentive to apply for as many slots as possible – both for direct use and to pre-empt one another and thereby store slots in space for future use. The outcome is an excessive filing for slots and as a result a large number of 'paper' satellites over Europe. Furthermore, as governments have locked up space locations for future use, there is at present a shortage of space capacity for new private entrants.

Of course, the current allocation mechanism could be improved by allowing for temporary leases of slots (to the extent that this is technically feasible – the lifetime of a satellite cannot be fully controlled). This would allow the current shortage of capacity to disappear, but the incentive for excessive filing and possible abuse of dominant position towards private users would remain.

Partly as a result of the current allocation of space locations, and in the absence of central coordination, national governments have also had an incentive to undertake their own space operations. In this respect as well, competition among national telecommunications operators (TOs) entails significant costs. TOs from France, the UK, Germany, Italy and Spain have launched their own satellites. Resources from different TOs have also been pooled in EUTELSAT, which is a cooperative of national telecom operators. The result is that a large number of operators have emerged, with each operating a small number of satellites, well below the minimum efficient scale of operations, which involves a stock of about ten satellites (Neven, Röller and Waverman, 1993).

In turn, the profitability of these small-scale operations has been maintained by their exercise of market power towards end-users. There have been national restrictions on the marketing of space capacity to prevent end-users from buying capacity outside the country in which they are located. Röller and Waverman (1991) estimate that the cost of fragmenting space operations in 1991, relative to a configuration involving fewer firms each operating at the minimum efficient scale, amounted to some 200 million ECU. Prices for access to space capacity

Table 7.2: Deregulation of the Satellite Industry: Estimated Welfare Changes. Million ECU.

Number of Operators	4	6	8	10
Welfare change (compared to no deregulation)	270	240	160	190
Collective losses of operators	–	162	301	428

Source: Neven, Röller and Waverman (1993).

are some 30–40% above those in the United States (Neven, Röller and Waverman, 1993).

The Commission's green paper on satellite communications proposes that the allocation of space locations should be coordinated at the EC level (possibly organized by competitive auctions) and that access to the space sector for end-users should be liberalized. In such an environment, one would expect competition between operators to be enhanced. Prices should fall and the demand for space capacity should increase, which in turn might allow a larger number of players to operate around the minimum efficient scale. A simple simulation projected to the year 2000 suggests that prices would indeed fall by some 30%. However, despite the increased demand, it turns out that only four operators could break even. Table 7.2 indicates that the benefits from deregulation would be reduced by some 30 million ECU if the current six operators stayed in the industry. They would incur total losses of about 160 million ECU.

Whether exit could occur at the appropriate pace without coordination is not clear. Some consolidation of the remaining players should therefore be strongly encouraged. However, the majority of these players are government owned; some may have deep pockets and their operations may not necessarily respond to strict financial criteria. By running unprofitable operations (at sub-optimal scale), these firms will impose an external cost on other operators, which cannot reach an adequate scale either. It is likely that this externality could only be properly internalized by a supranational authority. Indeed, some additional public operators (ITALSAT, HISPASAT) have indicated their intention to enter the industry, so that the prospect of eight independent operators is not unrealistic. If so, the industry would sustain losses of more than 300 million ECUs, and about 40% of the overall benefits of deregulating the industry would be wiped out.

The European Commission actually has the power (under Articles 90–92 of the Treaty of Rome) to investigate and (in some cases) curb the amounts of state aid. Unfortunately, satellite operations do not clearly fall under the scope of this Article. To extend it to comprise satellites could be a useful way of ensuring an efficient consolidation.

All in all, the case for a truly coordinated solution to the problem of achieving scale economies in European satellite operations is very strong. It seems very unlikely that cooperation rather than centralization can work. Implausibly large benefits from the greater accountability of regulatory authorities at the national level would be needed to outweigh these considerations. The presumption here is clearly in favour of a central authority.

7.6   Concluding Remarks

Our illustrations of the subsidiarity principle in this chapter have produced recommendations that were highly dependent on the circumstances of the particular case. In many regulatory areas – with the notable exception of drinking water regulation – we see significant merit in centralized or partially centralized policies, and in many respects the Community's current practices are well thought out. But one striking conclusion of the chapter is that two of the areas in which the case for centralization of EC power is weakest are the two which currently represent the largest components of the Community's budget. The problems of agriculture are well known. We have stressed that our scepticism about centralization of EC powers in the field of regional policy is compatible with an important role for the EC in coordinating the policy of its member states, and this role may make itself visible in the form of large budgetary resources that are administered (even if not controlled) by the Community. But these observations suggest that the principle of subsidiarity, if taken seriously, warrants a major rethinking of the Community's current spending priorities. The case for centralization appears to be strongest in areas whose budgetary requirements are not high and weakest in those where the budgetary cost is large.

Notes

[1] Larre (1990) claims that 'every European citizen deserves the same level of protection.' In the Water for Human Consumption Directive, and others, the Council comes very close to making this argument its own when it argues that common standards are necessary in order to provide for the 'harmonious development of economic activities'.

[2] 'Rhine plan gets seal of approval', *World Water and Environmental Engineer*, March 1992. The fact that salmon has not actually returned does not disprove his claim as its passage is still blocked by dams at a number of points. Ladders are planned.

[3] In theory, cash payments by France to the Netherlands could have solved the problem, but such solutions are often hard to implement.

[4] It would clearly be preferable to tackle this kind of distortion directly as part of the reform of the Common Agricultural Policy. (This might include, as an interim measure, raising prices for fertilizer so that its price relative to final output was less distorted than at present.) How realistic this is can be left for the reader to decide.

[5] Newbery (1990) discusses proposals for decentralized solutions to the problem of acid rain, including tradable emissions permits. He emphasizes that uniform reductions in emissions can be highly inefficient.

[6] Source: *The Community Budget: the Facts in Figures,* 3rd edition, 1990. Table 1 ('The overall size of the Community budget since the outset').

[7] This section draws on Krugman and Venables (1990).

8 Concluding Remarks

This Report has tried to make sense of subsidiarity as a criterion for the allocation of power within the European Community. The subsidiarity principle is not just a call for decentralization. It accepts that centralization may make sense when there are benefits to member states in pursuing cooperative policies, and when coordination between fully sovereign countries to achieve these benefits has little credibility, because of circumstances that make it hard for each of them to resist the temptation to pursue more self-interested policies. But centralization has a cost: the risk of government failure, which may be more severe for centralized policies because of the diminished accountability of the centre to the diverse needs of local people and communities.

Accountability is a notion that economics has often ignored, not because it is unimportant but because it is hard to analyse systematically. We have argued that progress in analysing accountability is possible, and the growing scholarly and public awareness in recent years of the nature of government failure and the weaknesses of public choice mechanisms is a good place to start. It is particularly important to do so, otherwise we risk allowing the benefits of centralization (which often arise due to spillovers and other phenomena that can be quantified) to drive policy conclusions without due attention to the costs, which are typically harder to measure. The swing in the European political mood in the last two or three years against centralization – of which the emphasis on subsidiarity is one expression – owes something to justified concerns that an issue of great importance has for too long been ignored.

The fact that this Report shares these concerns has not led us to argue everywhere against centralization. In many fields – competition policy, industrial restructuring, some kinds of environmental regulation, for example – application of the principles we have analysed makes us willing, even enthusiastic centralizers. We have also argued that the case for centralizing many of the basic provisions of the modern welfare state, which is not yet a strong one, could become much stronger if large-scale legal immigration into Europe dramatically increases the mobility of labour among the EC's member states. But in two respects at least our conclusions may strike many readers as strongly anti-centralist. The first is that we see no case for centralizing policies on social protection and workers' rights. Individual countries may choose levels of workers' protection that are as generous as they please, but the fear of 'social dumping' provides at present no reason for the Community to take that choice on their behalf. The second is that, on balance, the policies for which the case for centralization is strongest are not those that will make large claims on the Community budget. By contrast, those where the case is weakest include the most expensive items of all: agricultural spending and the Social and Regional Funds. Our conclusions may not, in the aggregate, imply that the balance of Community and member states' power should be very different from what it is at present. But they certainly imply that the Community budget should be no larger than it is now. If the EC needs to rescue the hard-pressed welfare state from the hands of its members, that judgement may change; but we are not there yet.

Our scepticism about centralization may seem to give comfort to those who, in terms of the current political debate, characterize themselves as anti-federalist. But we are not anti-federalists, and describing the debate as one between federalism and anti-federalism is misleading. Our concern to clarify subsidiarity springs precisely from the awareness that the European Community is already in essential respects a federal state in all but name. Unlike most federations, however, it has not come to terms with that fact. A clear statement of the principles of subsidiarity, and an open attempt to ensure the Community has procedures and institutions that can put it coherently into practice, are all the more necessary now that the key steps to federation have already been taken.

References

Aghion, P and P Bolton (1992), 'An Incomplete Contracts Approach to Financial Contracting', *Review of Economic Studies*, vol. 59, pp. 473-94.

Bayoumi, T and P Masson (1993), 'Fiscal Policy in the United States and Canada: Lessons from Monetary Union in Europe', unpublished paper, April.

Bewley, T F (1981), 'A Critique of Tiebout's Theory of Local Public Expenditures', *Econometrica*, pp. 713-40.

Börsch-Supan, A (1991), 'Aging Population: Problems and Policy Options in the US and Germany', *Economic Policy*, 12, April, pp. 103-39.

Brennan, G and J M Buchanan (1980), *The Power to Tax: Analytical Foundations of a Fiscal Constitution*, Cambridge University Press, Cambridge

Breton, A (1987), 'Towards a Theory of Competitive Federalism', *European Journal of Political Economy*, Special Issue, vol. 3, nos. 1 and 2.

Buckwell, A E, D R Harvey, K J Thomson and K A Parton (1982), *The Cost of the Common Agricultural Policy*, Croom Helm, London.

CEPR (1992), *Is Bigger Better? The Economics of EC Enlargement*, Third Annual Report of a Panel of CEPR Research Fellows on Monitoring European Integration, Centre for Economic Policy Research, London.

Dafflon, B (1990), 'Intergovernmental Equalization in Switzerland', unpublished, University of Fribourg, August.

Deaton, A and J Muellbauer (1980), 'An Almost Ideal Demand System', *American Economic Review*, vol. 70, pp. 312-26.

Dewatripont, M and J Tirole (1993), 'A Theory of Debt and Equity: Diversity of Securities and Manager–Shareholder Congruence', unpublished paper.

Drèze, J (1993), 'Regions of Europe: A Feasible Status, to be Discussed', *Economic Policy*, 17, October, pp. 266-307.

Drèze, J and E Malinvaud (1993), 'Growth and Employment – The Scope for a European Initiative', mimeo, Center for Operations Research and Econometrics, Louvain-la-Neuve.

Duff, A (ed.) (1993), *Subsidiarity Within the European Community*, The Federal Trust, London.

Edwards, J and M Keen (1993), 'Leviathan and Tax Competition', unpublished paper.

Eichengreen, B (1990), 'One Money for Europe: Conceptual Issues and Lessons from the US Currency Union', *Economic Policy*, 10, April, pp. 117-87.

EC (1992), *Mobility and Social Cohesion in the EC*, Office for Official Publications of the European Communities, Luxembourg.

Farnham, P G (1986), 'The Median Voter Model: Does Form of Government Matter?', mimeo, Georgia State University, Atlanta, GA.

Gatsios, K and P Seabright (1989), 'Regulation in the European Community', *Oxford Review of Economic Policy*, vol. 5, no. 2, pp. 37-60.

HM Treasury (1988), 'Taxation in the Single Market: A Market-based Approach', Press release, 8 September.

Hirschman, A (1970), *Exit, Voice and Loyalty*, Harvard University Press, Cambridge, MA.

House of Lords (1989), 'Fraud Against the Community', 5th Report, Select Committee on the European Communities, Session 1988-9, HMSO, London.

Italianer, A and J Pisani-Ferry (1992), 'Regional Stabilization Properties of Fiscal Arrangements: What Lessons for the Community?' unpublished paper, June.

Kovar, R (1990), 'Compétences des communautés', *Europe fasc. 420. Droit international fasc. 161-32*, Editions Techniques – Juris-Classeurs.

Krugman, P and A Venables (1990), 'Integration and the Competitiveness of Peripheral Industry', in Bliss, C and J Braga de Macedo (eds.), *Unity with Diversity in the European Economy: The Community's Southern Frontier, Cambridge University Press, Cambridge.*

Laffont, J-J and J Tirole (1993), *A Theory of Incentives in Procurement and Regulation*, MIT Press, Cambridge, MA.

Larre, D (1990), 'Les eaux en Europe: Etats et politique', *Courants*, no. 5, Special Issue, September-October, pp. 80-84.

McEachern, W A (1978), 'Collective Decision Rules and Local Debt Choice: A Test of the Median Voter Hypothesis', *National Tax Journal*, vol. 31, no. 2, pp. 129-36.

Mélitz, J and S Vori (1992), 'National Insurance Against Unevenly Distributed Shocks in a European Monetary Union', CEPR Discussion Paper No. 697, Centre for Economic Policy Research, London, August.

Neven, D, R Nuttall and P Seabright (1993), *Merger in Daylight: The Economics and Politics of European Merger Control*, Centre for Economic Policy Research, London.

Neven, D, L-H Röller and L Waverman (1993), 'Sunk in Space: The Economics of the European Satellite Industry and Prospects for Liberalization', *Economic Policy*, 17, October, pp. 401-32.

Newbery, D (1990), 'Acid Rain', *Economic Policy*, 11, October, pp. 297-346.

Nöhrbass, K-H and M Raab (1990), 'Quellensteuer und Kapitalmarkt', *Finanzarchiv*, vol. 48, pp. 179-93.

OECD (1990), 'Modelling the Effects of Agricultural Policies', *OECD Economic Studies*, no. 13, Organisation for Economic Co-operation and Development, Paris.

Pommerehne, W W (1974), 'Determinanten öffentliche Ausgaben: Ein einfaches politischökonomisches Modell', *Schweizerische Zeitschrift für Volkswirtschaft und Statistik*, 110, no. 3, pp. 455-91.

Pommerehne, W W (1977), 'Quantitative Aspects of Federalism: A Study of Six Countries', in Oates, W E (ed.), *The Political Economy of Fiscal Federalism*, Heath, Lexington, pp. 275-355.

Pommerehne, W W (1983), 'Private versus öffentliche Müllabfuhr – nochmals betrachtet', *Finanzarchiv*, 41, no. 2, pp. 466-75.

Pommerehne, W W (1990), 'Empirical Relevance of Comparative Institutional Analysis', *European Economic Review*, 34, pp. 458-69.

Pommerehne, W W and G Kirchgässner (1993), 'Etat fédératif et dépenses publiques: une analyse économétrique comparative', Cahiers de Recherche, Faculté des Sciences Economiques, Université de la Sarre, C 9301, March.

References 165

Röller, L-H and L Waverman (1991), 'The Optimal Structure of the European Satellite Operations Industry', mimeo, INSEAD, Fontainebleau.

Rosenthal, D E (1990), 'Competition Policy', in Hufbauer, G C (ed.), *Europe 1992: An American Perspective*, The Brookings Institution, Washington DC.

Santerre, R (1986), 'Representative versus Direct Democracy: A Tiebout Test of Relative Performance', *Public Choice*, vol. 48, no. 1, pp. 55-63.

Seabright, P (1993), 'Decentralization and Accountability: An Incomplete Contracts Model', unpublished paper.

Simon, G (1991), 'Une Europe Communautaire de moins en moins mobile', *Revue Européenne des Migrations Internationales*, vol. 7, no. 2.

Sinn, H-W (1987), *Capital Income Taxation and Resource Allocation*, North-Holland Publishing Co., Amsterdam, New York, Oxford and Tokyo.

Stigler, G (1971), 'The Theory of Economic Regulation', *Bell Journal of Economics*, vol. 2, pp. 3-21.

Stragier, J (1993), 'The Competition Rules of the EEA Agreement and their Implementation', *European Competition Law Review*, vol. 14, pp. 30-8.

Tiebout, C M (1956), 'A Pure Theory of Local Expenditures', *Journal of Political Economy*, vol. 74, October, pp. 416-24.

Vandersanden, G (1992), 'Considérations sur le principe de subsidiarité', mimeo, Institut d'Etudes Européennes, Université Libre de Bruxelles.

von Weizsäcker, C C (1987), 'Föderalismus als Verjüngunskur', in Buhofer, H (ed.), *Liberalismus als Verjüngunskur*, Orell Füssli, Zürich, pp. 217-35.

Winters, L A (1987), 'The Economic Consequences of Agricultural Support: A Survey', *OECD Economic Studies*, no. 9, Autumn, pp. 7-54, Organisation for Economic Co-operation and Development, Paris.

Winters, L A (1988), 'Completing the European Internal Market: Some Notes on Trade Policy', *European Economic Review*, vol. 32, pp. 1477-99.

Winters, L A (1991), 'Digging for Victory: Agricultural Protection and National Security', *The World Economy*, vol. 13, pp. 170-90.